# DEAL *Diva*

how to negotiate your way to success
without selling your soul

# DEAL *Diva*

how to negotiate
your way to success
without selling
your soul

KIM MEREDITH

Published by Zebra Press
an imprint of Random House Struik (Pty) Ltd
Company Reg. No. 1966/003153/07
80 McKenzie Street, Cape Town, 8001
PO Box 1144, Cape Town, 8000, South Africa

www.zebrapress.co.za

First published 2010

1 3 5 7 9 10 8 6 4 2

Publication © Zebra Press 2010
Text © Kim Meredith 2010

Cover image: Getty Images/Amy Gulp

All rights reserved. No part of this publication may be reproduced, stored in a retrieval system or transmitted, in any form or by any means, electronic, mechanical, photocopying, recording or otherwise, without the prior written permission of the copyright owners.

PUBLISHER: Marlene Fryer
MANAGING EDITOR: Ronel Richter-Herbert
PROOFREADER: Beth Housdon
COVER AND TEXT DESIGNER: Monique Oberholzer
TYPESETTER: Monique van den Berg
PRODUCTION MANAGER: Valerie Kömmer

Set in 11 pt on 15 pt Minion

Printed and bound by Pinetown Printers, Pinetown, KwaZulu-Natal

ISBN 978 1 77020 039 5

Over 50 000 unique African images available to purchase
from our image bank at www.imagesofafrica.co.za

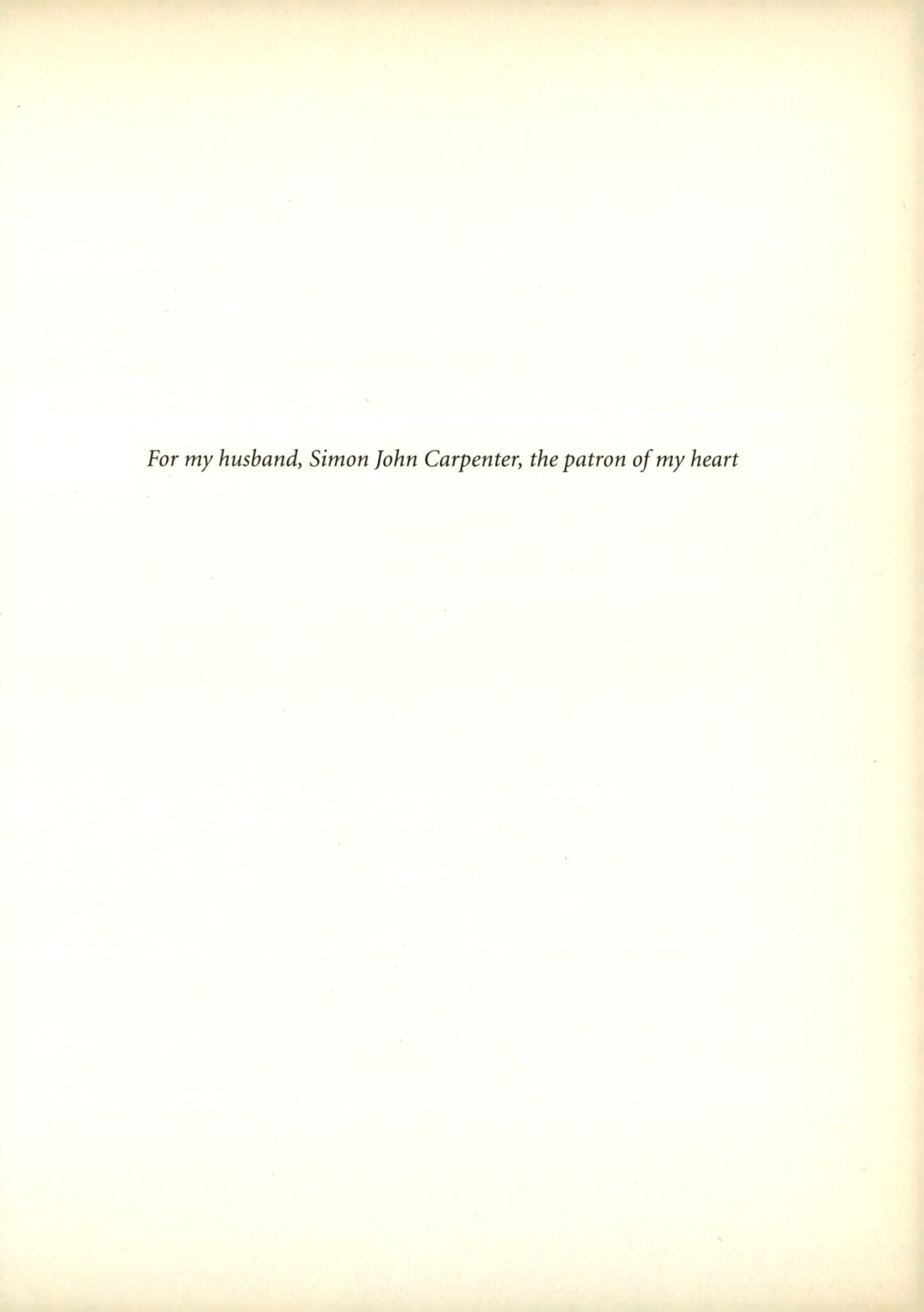

*For my husband, Simon John Carpenter, the patron of my heart*

# Contents

ACKNOWLEDGEMENTS ................................................................. xi
ABOUT THE AUTHOR .................................................................. xiii
INTRODUCTION ............................................................................. 1

## 1 > ARE YOU A DIVA OR A DOORMAT? .................................. 5
The Doormat and the Victim ............................................................ 7
The Diva and the Goddess ............................................................. 16
When Women Became Workers .................................................... 21

## 2 > DIVAS GET WHAT THEY DESERVE ................................. 25
Why Are Women Getting a Dodgy Deal? ...................................... 31
Value, Negotiation and Prostitution ............................................... 32
How to Value You ............................................................................ 34
How to Value the Work That You Do ............................................. 34
Value and the Bigger Picture ......................................................... 45
One Flaw in Women ....................................................................... 48

## 3 > FROM DIVA TO DEAL DIVA ............................................... 50
Lessons from Children in Dealmaking .......................................... 51
Selling, Persuading and Pleading .................................................. 54
Negotiating, Horse-trading and Compromising Positions .......... 56
A Catalogue of Choices .................................................................. 59
What Makes Negotiation So Special? ........................................... 66
Is Everything Negotiable? .............................................................. 69
Do You Get What You Deserve, or Deserve What You Get? ...... 71
Discombobulated, Dearest? ........................................................... 75

## 4 > WOMEN AND THE FINE ART OF COMMUNICATION ... 77
Conscious Verbal Communication – What Women Say ... 80
Unconscious Verbal Communication – What Women Mean ... 82
Body Language – What Women Suggest ... 85
Esoteric Communication, Gut Instinct, Feminine Intuition ... 86
The Debating Society ... 88
The Danger of Debate ... 94
A Lesson in Communication ... 96

## 5 > THE POWER AND THE GLORY ... 97
Creating Power from the Almost-empty Pantry ... 99
Getting Your Negotiating Gear Engaged ... 100
The Power of Planning ... 101
The Power of Carrots ... 111
Who Really, Really Needs the Deal? ... 113
Perceptions of You ... 114
Language and Word Power ... 118
Negotiating from a Weak Position ... 118
Don't Mess With a Diva ... 120

## 6 > BEING THE DIVA YOU ARE MEANT TO BE ... 121
Determining the Styles ... 122
Describing the Different Styles ... 125
Your Behavioural Style and Your Negotiating Style ... 133
Be True to Who You Are ... 138

## 7 > HOW TO DEFINE THE DEAL YOU WANT ... 139
Have a Strategy for *How* to Get What You Want ... 140
Use a Process to Define *What* Deal You Want ... 142
Step 1: The Issues ... 142
Step 2: The Ball Park ... 145

Step 3: The Players ................................................................ 151
The Lawyer and the Duck ..................................................... 157

## 8 > HOW TO NEGOTIATE FACE TO FACE ...................... 159
The Power of the Proposal ..................................................... 160
Who Should Make the First Move? ........................................ 160
The First Proposal .................................................................. 162
The Art of Propositioning ...................................................... 164
Strictly Come Dancing ........................................................... 166
When Someone Says 'No' ..................................................... 168
To Walk Away or Not to Walk Away? .................................... 170
Guidelines for Engagement .................................................... 171
When Enough Is Enough ....................................................... 172
How to Woo Friends and Win Family .................................... 175
On Getting Your Own Way ..................................................... 176

## 9 > REAL-LIFE DEAL DIVAS ............................................. 178
Joan Joffe .............................................................................. 179
Kate Rau ................................................................................ 182
Elizabeth Malumo ................................................................. 185
Jenna Clifford ........................................................................ 187
Professor Shirley Zinn ........................................................... 190
Terry Dearling ....................................................................... 192
Christine Williams ................................................................. 195
Deborah 'Debbie' Lefebvre .................................................... 197
Personal Growth ................................................................... 201

## 10 > THE END IS THE BEGINNING ................................... 203
A Summary of Everything ..................................................... 203

## PINA COLADAS AND CHERRIES ...................................... 213
## REFERENCES ..................................................................... 215

# Acknowledgements

It never ceases to amaze me how many people are willing to help. Advice, guidance, compliments, criticisms, anecdotes, sharing lessons and souls, cooking, chasing – you name it. It is my privilege to thank each and every one of you.

Let me begin with my husband, Simon Carpenter, who is the husband we all dream of having – a man who loves unconditionally, lavishes heartfelt praise, is willing to share his life and his love, cooks like a super chef (*and* cleans up after himself!) and genially ignores me when I am being impossible.

My fabulous friends. With little in the way of relatives and zero in the way of children, my friends are a vital part of my family. They offer everything one expects from people (but usually only gets from dogs) – loyalty, love, generosity, endless support and forgiveness (so please forgive me if I have not mentioned your name!). My profound appreciation to Brenda Bensted-Smith, Stacey Bossenger, Barbara Edwards, Karen Evans, *Thin Cow* Cathrine Moncur, Brenda Smee, Cherylynn Smee (now Johnson) and Chris van der Walt. Thank you for allowing me to be part of your pack.

Ashley Marchment, who even offered to write for me if I was going to miss my deadline. You are a honey, Ash, and a remarkable friend.

To the world-class negotiators and dealmakers who inspired, and still inspire, me to chase the perfect deal – Joan Joffe, Nic Frangos and Gary Harlow. Thank you for being willing to mentor and guide some rather raw but keen material.

To Stephen White, John McMillan and the team at Scotwork who, early on in my career, taught me how to teach the best negotiating skills across the globe.

The wonderful women, divas all, who were kind enough to be interviewed for this book – Joan Joffe, Kate Rau, Elizabeth Malumo, Jenna Clifford, Shirley Zinn, Terry Dearling, Christine Williams and Debbie Lefebvre. Not forgetting, of course, Nicola Jackson (now Coetzer) and Catie Louw. Helping other women assures you all of your special place in heaven.

Julie Purkis, Harley-Davidson owner, business partner and friend – what would I do without you? You are a perfect balance of selflessness and control. Thank you for clearing my desk and running the business while I wrote. Thank you for the encouragement and informal editing, and for being such a brilliant publicist and marketer. You are worth your *Thin Cow* weight in gold.

To the support system I lean on, sometimes rather heavily, but who keep me in one piece – buy a donkey. Sharon 'Shaz' Maxwell, the *Thin Cow* who was my left arm and right arm during the writing process. Matrina Ngcobo, our amazing housekeeper, who runs our home with calmness, efficiency and polish. Jean Slaughter, for helping with some rather urgent personal errands.

A special word of thanks to my parents, John and Colleen Meredith, who love me even when I am so focused that I can't have a decent conversation on the phone. Dad, you have put up with my schemes and dreams and general dealing since I was a very junior diva. How can I ever repay you?

Lastly and especially to Ronel Richter-Herbert and Marlene Fryer of Zebra Press for their faith in me. No author could ever wish for a more encouraging yet non-intrusive publishing team. Champagne! In Paris?

# About the Author

Kim Meredith is an internationally acclaimed lecturer, sales strategist, negotiator and dealmaker. Kim is chief executive officer of the globally represented The Dealmaker Programmes Company based in Mauritius.

Having held executive positions in business since the late 1980s, Kim was one of only 179 women on the boards of the top 300 Johannesburg Stock Exchange (JSE)–listed companies by 2000.

Kim's most recent corporate position was with a listed information technology group, where she spent four years on the board as executive director of strategy. During this time, she was responsible for global strategy, including actively driving negotiations for strategic mergers, acquisitions and disposals.

Kim currently lectures and consults in negotiation and dealmaking in the USA, Latin America, Europe and Africa. She has been working with and consulting to international companies for over fifteen years.

Although Kim holds a BA degree in clinical psychology and English, she claims she would be a rubbish psychologist on account of her penchant for dispensing unsolicited advice. This shameless telling of people what to do resulted in her first book, *Work Diva: How to Climb the Corporate Ladder Without Selling Your Soul*, which was published in South Africa in January 2009.

# Introduction

How often do you lie in bed at night wishing, praying or hoping that something you really want will come to you? What about saying affirmations or thinking positive thoughts? How much of what you have wished for has materialised? Been a bit disappointed? Has this disillusionment stopped you from dreaming? Imagine, now, that you are given the power to control your life and to help you get what you want. Well, you are actually holding that power in your hands.

*Deal Diva: How to Negotiate Your Way to Success without Selling Your Soul* will show you how you can get what you want – well, most of it at any rate – without turning into a witch, a bitch or a nag. *Deal Diva* is different from the books on affirmations or the laws of attraction. This is a book about 'how' – how to change your destiny by relying on yourself and taking control of the situations that occur in your life every day. It doesn't matter whether you are buying (or selling) a house, a car or a business, negotiating the salary you want or getting your child to go to bed at night, this is a book on how you, as a woman, can do deals using negotiation – and a little bit of persuasion – to get what *you* want.

If the very word 'negotiation' fills you with dread and panic, take a deep breath. *Deal Diva* is not your normal boring business book. *Deal Diva* is about putting the power back (yes, *back*) into your hands by showing you how empowered women use negotiation in the real world. It's also about helping you to rediscover and develop the talents with which you were born so that you can improve your fortunes – in your business life *and* your personal life – forever.

Unfortunately, many women believe that they can't negotiate; that negotiation is a weapon used by hard-nosed businesspeople (usually men) to close important financial deals, or by policy-makers to conclude global agreements, or by governments to end (or provoke) wars. Negotiation *is* the skill of choice in these situations, but everyone uses negotiation every single day – and so do you. Think about it: What do you say to a friend to convince her to go out with you when she would rather stay at home? How do you get your sister to lend you her car (or dress, or money)? What do you offer your children in exchange for them eating their vegetables? These are all negotiated deals, and you do them without thinking twice. So why is it that when it comes to negotiation in a business context or looking after their own interests women seem to fall apart at the seams?

Women do no end of harm when they tell themselves that they can't negotiate (or 'do deals' as one says in the business world). This is when a woman becomes a doormat instead of a liberated, divine diva. *Everyone* needs to be able to negotiate – even the most powerful people in the world – in order to get what they really want in life. And so do you.

Here's the good news: Negotiation and dealmaking are *fun*. By the end of this book you will be itching to go out and make deals – with your husband, lover, mother, children, boss, employees … even the taxman! *Deal Diva* is a practical handbook that gives you the ability to become an awesome 'deal diva' – to balance assertiveness and aggression, to distinguish between what you want and what you need, to recognise your abilities and limitations, and to be self-sufficient.

The book is divided, roughly, into four sections:
1. *Why* women get less than they deserve.
2. *What* women need to know to become better dealmakers.
3. *How* women can become gifted negotiators.
4. *Wow!* To celebrate being a dazzling deal diva.

# INTRODUCTION

*Deal Diva* is the guide to negotiation that you will wish you had owned years ago. If you'd had it then, you might now have been on an island in the Caribbean sipping pina coladas. But, instead, you've been trampled on, taken for granted, paid less than you deserve, ignored or overlooked.

If you are reading this somewhere less exotic than a Caribbean beach, like in bed or sitting on your couch, don't feel too bad – this is the first step to changing your life and getting what *you've* always wanted. By the end of your journey with *Deal Diva*, you will be the diva and not the doormat. So, dear diva, go make yourself a pina colada, get comfortable and start reading about how you can change your destiny!

Recipe for the best (and easiest) pina colada

- 150 ml light rum
- 150 ml dark rum
- One tin crushed pineapple (which you need to crush some more)
- One tin coconut milk

1. Combine ingredients and shake well over lots of crushed ice
2. Decorate with a maraschino cherry
3. Add a few drops of cherry syrup to sweeten, if required

Kim Meredith
kimm@thedealmaker.com

## Chapter 1

## ARE YOU A DIVA OR A DOORMAT?

> 'There are only two types of women: goddesses and doormats.'
> – Pablo Picasso (Spanish painter; 1881–1973)

If you read my first book, *Work Diva: How to Climb the Corporate Ladder without Selling Your Soul*, you will already be familiar with this quote. If you haven't read *Work Diva* and thought the words 'diva' and 'doormat' in the Introduction to this book were randomly chosen words, you now know better. If you are horrified that such a sexist sentiment seems to be the basis of *Deal Diva*, please don't throw the book down in horror – give me a moment to explain.

This quote *is* somewhat one-dimensional, but the reason I love it is because it drives the following point home rather bluntly: *If you don't rise above being a victim, you can't expect to be treated as anything more than a doormat.* This is particularly true in the cut and thrust of business. You might be saying to yourself that surely there is something in between doormat and goddess. Perhaps there is, but let me ask you a question or two: Do you really want to be 'in between'? Do you want to be the middle, the average, the insipid shade of beige? Me neither. Embrace the possibility of being a fabulous diva, and you are already halfway there!

Before you can begin to release the awesome deal diva that I assure you is just beneath the surface, we need to check the extent to which you may have developed a victim mindset. While this might seem like a negative place to start, recognising whether you really see yourself as a goddess or a doormat is a vital first step. You might be absolutely certain that you are no victim, but often doormat mentality creeps up on women without them even noticing it. In order to ensure that you get the most you can from this book, it is important to identify the degree to which you allow yourself to be used as a doormat. You will then also know what needs to be done to banish the doormat and set your inner diva free.

Women in general seem to readily accept the expectations society imposes on them – that they nurture the children, make the sandwiches, sacrifice their own careers for the family or run around after bosses, provide the shoulder to cry on, keep the house tidy, do the cooking and cleaning, take a man's name. How much has really changed in the last 100 years?

Are you already starting to think about what is expected of you and how you accept this without question? Good! While I am not suggesting you suddenly stop doing these things for the people in your life, I want you to be aware of what you do, and why, as understanding this is a very important part of the process. You may even enjoy the tasks, but that doesn't mean they should not be valued by you, or by the people for whom you do them. ('Value' is a subject that we will explore with plenty of passion, but let's park it for a moment.)

If the definition of a doormat is someone who mindlessly does stuff expected of her without questioning why, what does it mean to be a diva? Do you think of a diva as a demanding, pushy, self-important bitch? Are you finding it a little difficult to picture yourself as a diva? The word 'diva' has traditionally suffered negative connotations, but take a quick look at http://thesaurus.reference.com/browse/diva. There is not a single bad synonym for 'diva'.

According to the *Collins Concise Dictionary Plus*, a 'diva' is defined as 'a highly distinguished female singer; prima donna (from the Latin "a goddess from *divus*")'. A 'goddess' is described by *Collins* as 'a female divinity; a woman who is adored or idealised', while a 'doormat' is 'a person who offers little resistance to ill-treatment'. Do you want to be someone who is adored and admired (even if only by yourself), or are you happy being the woman who offers little resistance to ill-treatment – the victim, in other words? Only you can choose.

## THE DOORMAT AND THE VICTIM

The *Collins* definition of a 'victim' is 'a person or thing that suffers harm'. A *'thing'*? Well, I guess a doormat *is* a thing, and it suffers because it offers little resistance to ill-treatment. With this in mind, you no doubt appreciate why the words 'victim' and 'doormat' are used interchangeably in this book. While I'm sure nobody wants to describe herself as a victim, and bearing in mind how easily a woman can slip into doormat mode, let's check how much of a victim frame of mind *you* have.

Other than the obvious 'yes' and 'no' responses, if your answer is 'occasionally' or 'not really', then tick the 'no' box. If your answer is 'probably' or 'mostly', then tick the 'yes' box. Don't stress too much when you see your results, as you do get another chance to take the test. Ready?

| THE VICTIM QUIZ | YES | NO |
|---|---|---|
| 1. Do you have poor self-esteem or lack confidence? | | |
| 2. When you look in the mirror, do you dislike what you see? | | |
| 3. Do other people put you down or treat you unfairly? | | |
| 4. Is someone else responsible for what goes wrong in your life? | | |
| 5. Are your 'rights' very important to you? | | |
| 6. Is discrimination (race, religion, gender, age, ability) or any other inequality the reason you don't have what you want? | | |
| 7. Are the government's policies (now or in the past) responsible for your not getting ahead? | | |
| 8. If you were thinner or more attractive (or taller or bigger or smaller), would your life be easier? | | |
| 9. If you were better connected (or born or married into a privileged family), would you be more successful? | | |
| 10. Has your lack of education held you back from achieving? | | |

DEAL *Diva*

| THE VICTIM QUIZ | YES | NO |
|---|---|---|
| 11. Have you had a hard life (abuse, abandonment, violence, crime, accident, disability) from which you can't recover emotionally? | | |
| 12. Do you think that bad luck or the spiritual path you have chosen has played a role in your misfortunes? | | |

If you have:
- Three or fewer 'yes' ticks, you are not a victim. In fact, you probably already realise your potential as a diva.
- Four to six 'yes' ticks, you are inclined to behave like a doormat from time to time, but you can quite as easily become a diva.
- Seven to nine 'yes' ticks, you are leaning towards being a victim, but you are not beyond redemption. By changing your attitude now, you can still reverse this trend.
- Ten to twelve 'yes' ticks, you are the classic victim. People will already have said this to you. Start believing that you *do* have choices in how you deal with life, and you will see your path slowly begin to change.

Bad news? Okay, I admit it. The questions were biased to help flush out the doormat in anyone. The good news is that you will get plenty of guidance in *Deal Diva* from real-life, genuine goddesses on how to release your incredible inner diva. What they will share with you, along with their own scars, is that, no matter how much life has beaten you up, stomped on you and tossed you out with the trash, being a victim or a doormat is an *attitude*. And attitude is something that can be changed (with a little commitment, of course). Just ask Oprah Winfrey (*American television producer and philanthropist; 1954–*).

In case you are interested in understanding more about yourself in the context of the quiz, here is the background to each question you answered.

## THE VICTIM QUIZ ASSESSMENT

### 1. Do you have poor self-esteem or lack confidence?

It is perfectly normal to suffer from low self-esteem or a lack of confidence from time to time. If you find that you *continually* doubt yourself, you need to consider attending a course or participating in a programme that will help boost your self-image and self-assurance. Not wanting to fix your esteem issues is symptomatic of being a victim.

On the other hand, zero self-doubt and a super-sized confidence are indicators of low EQ (emotional intelligence). EQ is very different from IQ (intellectual intelligence). If you are someone who is *never* wrong, I would like to recommend that you spend some time reading books (containing self-development exercises) about increasing your emotional intelligence – and don't skip the exercises!

### 2. When you look in the mirror, do you dislike what you see?

All of us look in the mirror and find fault with some aspect of our bodies. We know we shouldn't, but we do. It is when you can't bear the sight of your own reflection (in a mirror or photo) that you have a real problem. Someone (a professional, not a friend or family member) needs to work through this with you. Not being able to look at yourself is closely linked to your self-esteem. Equally, looking in the mirror and thinking you are utterly perfect is linked to narcissism.

In either case, do yourself a favour and watch the movie *Last Holiday* with Queen Latifah (*born Dana Elaine Owens; American actress and singer; 1970–*). There is a wonderful scene in which Queen Latifah's character, Georgia Bird, talks to her reflection in the mirror. This is how we all need to be talking to ourselves – with a balance of pride and humility!

On the subject of humility and being a diva, I read a quote the other day that went something like, 'There is nothing as vain as false humility.' Indeed.

## THE VICTIM QUIZ ASSESSMENT

### 3. Do other people put you down or treat you unfairly?

Eleanor Roosevelt (*American humanitarian and First Lady; 1884–1962*) said, 'Nobody can make you feel inferior without your permission.' This truism works on two levels. What it means is, *firstly*, that if you believe others are putting you down or treating you unfairly, it is because you are literally allowing them to treat you in this way. Back to the mirror. How do you talk to yourself? Do you not think that if you talk badly to yourself, you are being a bit of a hypocrite when you're surprised that other people talk badly to you too? Stop being unkind to yourself and the people around you will stop being unkind to you. It sounds ridiculous, but that's exactly what happens – try it for yourself.

*Secondly*, the opposite of a victim is a cognisant, i.e. someone who is self-aware. And someone who is self-aware recognises that she can either accept being put down, or not. If you refuse to feel inferior – whether someone is actually diminishing you or not – you give that person no power over you. A victim relinquishes power. A diva says, 'Sod off and take your issues with you.'

### 4. Is someone else responsible for what goes wrong in your life?

Very few people don't blame others, even in a small way, for their problems. The more you blame factors other than yourself, the greater your inclination to be a victim. It is important to appreciate that being a victim or a doormat is an *attitude*, a chosen reality. Think about the stories you have read or seen on television about individuals overcoming horrific incidents in their lives. All these people have recovered emotionally (but not necessarily physically) from being 'victims' of the violence, crime or disability they suffered.

You already know that the first step in correcting any attitude or behaviour is *awareness*. From now on, this very minute, start being more aware of what you say and how you react when things go wrong. If you realise that

## THE VICTIM QUIZ ASSESSMENT

you are blaming other entities (be they people, events, circumstances, deities or your demographics – race, gender, age, wealth, etc.) instead of taking charge of your own life, you are allowing a victim attitude to prevail. To stop this behaviour, you need to go to the opposite extreme for a while. Take personal responsibility for fixing *everything* that happens to you, even when you *know* you are not to blame or at fault, and the victim mindset will automatically start disappearing.

### 5. Are your 'rights' very important to you?

If you marked 'yes' for this point, you may initially disagree that expecting rights is synonymous with being a victim, but hear me out. Imagine a world in which only children and animals (and trees) had 'rights' and every adult had 'responsibilities'. Imagine that we, as adults, were responsible for peace and harmony on the planet, for treating others with dignity, respect, compassion and fairness, for keeping our word and always telling the truth. I could go on and on, but I'm sure you get the picture. If we accepted these responsibilities, then nobody would need rights, not so?

Enough philosophising for the moment; back to doormats. As I said in *Work Diva*, people who have a 'rights' rather than a 'responsibilities' mentality tend not to do particularly well in life. These are not the people who rise to the top of their chosen lives – be it mother or managing director. Victimhood is all about 'me, me, me', and being too egocentric damages your relationship with those around you (and ultimately yourself). Give up your right to rights and accept your responsibility to be responsible.

### 6. Is discrimination (race, religion, gender, age, ability) or any other inequality the reason you don't have what you want?

I was presenting to a group of about thirty female lawyers recently and made the following statement: If you are blaming your sex, the colour of

## THE VICTIM QUIZ ASSESSMENT

your skin, your beliefs or whatever else for your problems, you are being a victim. Most of the women agreed, but after the lecture a young lady came up to me and said, 'I understand what you said, but I really *am* discriminated against because of my gender – and I'm *not* a victim.' She was by no means the first person to say something like this to me. I have had white people say that affirmative action has made it impossible for them to find jobs, and at the same time I've had black people say that discrimination still limits them in the workplace.

The point is that being a victim is a perception, an attitude. Every single person on the planet can say, 'It's because I'm *x* that I'm disadvantaged.' *Everyone* falls into some category or another (male/female, black/white, young/old, scrawny/fat, whatever/whichever) that makes them different from another group, yet not every person on the planet blames their category for their lot in life – only victims do. I'm not saying that discrimination does not exist – of course it does – but it is your attitude towards dealing with discrimination that makes you a diva or a doormat.

### 7. Are the government's policies (now or in the past) responsible for you not getting ahead?

Much like the comments above regarding discrimination, if you are blaming the government, you are being a victim. Every single group in history can blame another group for their circumstances. In her keynote speech for the Law Society of the Northern Province in September 2009, Graça Machel (*Former First Lady of Mozambique and South Africa; 1945–*) said, 'The problems in South Africa are not legislation; it's about attitudes, beliefs, value systems.'

The closest, perhaps, that we can get to a group who can't honestly blame anyone else is the Thais. Thailand has always been self-governing, but some Thais will probably point out that they were occupied by China and India

## THE VICTIM QUIZ ASSESSMENT

a thousand years ago. Where does it start and where does it end? It stops when we accept responsibility to take as much control over our lives as we can. And in the free world, we actually can.

### 8. If you were thinner or more attractive (or taller or bigger or smaller), would your life be easier?

Get in line, girl. All of us want to be thinner or prettier (or whatever). Look at the most successful people in the world. I wouldn't exactly call Oprah Winfrey 'skinny' or Bill Gates 'handsome'. There are very few perfect people in the world, yet there are millions of very successful people.

Changing some aspect of your physical being will probably not alter your lot in life. Sure, getting a nose job may make you feel better about yourself, which should help boost your confidence, but the essence of who you are remains the same. If you are a victim, whether beautiful or not, it just ain't gonna happen for you. (On the subject of nose jobs, you are *never* happy with the outcome.)

### 9. If you were better connected (or born or married into a privileged family), would you be more successful?

There is no denying that having old money connections or belonging to the right country club or having attended the right university will help your network – and being successful is all about networking. Equally, I'm sure that having lots of money makes being unsuccessful or unhappy a much more comfortable experience!

Using Oprah Winfrey as an example again: Here is a woman who could have complained that being female, black, poor, American and disadvantaged hampered her efforts to be successful. Oprah, however, believes: 'The greatest discovery of all time is that a person can change his future by merely changing his attitude.' Granted, we don't all have the heart of Oprah burning inside of us, but I bet that you can think of plenty of people who have

## THE VICTIM QUIZ ASSESSMENT

overcome less than salubrious beginnings to go on to make a success of their lives. For a South African example, just read about jeweller-artist Jenna Clifford's early life. Only victims blame their disadvantaged beginnings.

**10. Has your lack of education held you back from achieving?**
Like many other women I know, I grew up in an era when parents believed that women were destined for marriage, babies and happy ever after. I was a disinterested learner who didn't bother much with studying – probably because, in those days, girls only got teaching bursaries. I wanted to be a marine biologist, not a teacher! With no bursary, mediocre school results and zero cash, my only option was to start working. My first job was as a teller in a building society, but I soon found (to my surprise) that I was pretty ambitious and happy to work hard. Even though I had a management position by age twenty-three, I realised that I wasn't going to progress much further without a degree.

I registered with a distance-learning university and, despite being at my very supportive boss's behest twenty-four hours a day, I managed to obtain the degree. Did my degree make me smarter? A bit. Was it difficult to study *and* work (and play)? You betcha. Did it open doors? That it did. No one seemed to mind that it was a degree in English and clinical psychology, even when I found myself in the world of corporate finance. *I had a degree.* The biggest benefit, though, was to me as a person. Having a degree really boosted my confidence.

Perhaps if I'd had a private-school education or an Ivy League–university degree, other doors would have opened for me. But then again, I might have screwed it all up and had to start from scratch! Don't discount the 'university of hard knocks' (learning from experience) – fewer than half of the world's ten richest people completed their tertiary education (including Bill Gates, the richest person in the whole wide world).

## THE VICTIM QUIZ ASSESSMENT

**11. Have you had a hard life (abuse, abandonment, violence, crime, accident, disability) from which you can't recover emotionally?**
Every single person can tell you a hard-luck story. Each one of us has been damaged in some way – some more than others – but it is all relative. 'Relative to what?' you might ask. It's relative to the manner in which we choose to cope. There are enlightened people who will tell you that these hardships ultimately become a blessing; there are resilient people who pick themselves up, dust themselves off and move forward; there are those who learn from their traumas and become whole or help others – and then there are the victims.

You know that scene in *Notting Hill* (with Julia Roberts) where the dinner guests compete for the last brownie? (In case you don't, in the movie the person at the dinner table who tells the saddest tale about his or her life wins the last chocolate brownie on the plate.) Well, I win the brownie every time! Yet I still look at people born with severe disabilities or those who've suffered extreme violence and think how lucky I am. It's that 'relative' thing – if you, after all you've been through, can still look at other 'less fortunate' people and consider yourself blessed, then you are no doormat.

**12. Do you think that bad luck or the spiritual path you have chosen has played a role in your misfortunes?**
Cursing your luck, the universe or whatever force in which you choose to believe is a form of blame. See point 4 above. But if you are convinced that, from a spiritual point of view, you have chosen a path of suffering and that you have no choice but to suffer, then that is the path you will see laid out before you. Whatever your life path, you still have a choice to approach it with a diva frame of mind rather than that of a doormat.

Now that you have read the explanation for each point in the quiz, I suggest you redo the exercise. I am pretty sure that with just this little bit of insight, you will find that you now have fewer 'yes' ticks. Charles Darwin (*English naturalist and father of evolution; 1809–1882*) said, 'It is not the strongest of the species that survives, or the most intelligent, but the one most responsive to change.'

## THE DIVA AND THE GODDESS

Why do some women become doormats when it's just as easy for them to become divas? There are many reasons, but most commonly victim behaviour is triggered by something that has happened at a very early stage in the person's life. This victim behaviour then drives the person's attitude, which, in turn, defines the behaviour, which reinforces the attitude. Arguing about whether attitudes or behaviours develop first is a bit like the chicken and the egg debate.

Back to how women become doormats. Picture a child who is pushed over in the playground and falls and scrapes her knee. The teachers fuss over her and, when she gets home, her parents pay her more attention. The next week the child trips over some toys and hurts herself. Again she receives sympathy and affection. Then she is bullied, and the cycle repeats. Soon the child notices the pattern and starts to anticipate being upset in some way because she knows it will result in love and attention.

Without anyone realising it, the child is becoming a victim. She may start inventing little stories about how she has been hurt, or telling anyone who will listen about her sore finger or stubbed toe. Don't for a minute believe that children tell only the truth. They all lie, which means that all adults know how to lie too. Victimhood is built on lying to oneself, on unwittingly creating a set of beliefs and attitudes into which one buys.

If you want to question my assertion that all children lie, I'm delighted to hear it. You are starting to challenge the status quo. Hello, diva! It's true about the fibbing, by the way. Research conducted by Dr Richard Wiseman (*English psychology professor and researcher; 1966–*) and featured in the book *Quirkology: The Curious Science of Everyday Lives*, reveals that by age three 50 per cent of children tell fibs, and by the time they reach five *all* children lie. (If you want to read more on this subject, buy a copy of *Quirkology* – it's one of the most fascinating books ever.) I don't believe kids are being intentionally deceptive. I think they are creating an alternative reality for themselves – a world that they want.

You may ask: If victims can create their reality, can divas do the same thing? You've got it! *We are able to create the world in which we want to live.* Perception may be reality, but a reality – a truth – it is. And that means that if you want to change from being a doormat to being a diva, all you need to do is alter your reality. Change your perception, your attitude, your behaviour – don't get too hung up on the psychology. Just start with whichever is easiest for you.

Can you imagine what you could achieve by combining a new reality change with learning the negotiating skills and dealmaking expertise of brilliant businesspeople, powerful politicians and influential movie moguls? If you're still saying to yourself, 'I could never learn those things,' go back to the mirror and have a stern chat with your reflection about being a doormat. You *can* learn these things, because they are really not that difficult – and you've got *Deal Diva* in your hands to guide you. Are you ready to become a diva – a goddess who is adored?

## SIX STEPS TO BEING A DIVINE DIVA
### 1. You have the power to change your reality

By being aware of your doormat tendencies and believing you are worthy of being adored, you can become a goddess. All that's required is a small adjustment in reality. For example, stop the moaning and start counting your blessings. Just this one tiny shift in attitude and behaviour will change your world – and your life – forever. Start believing that you deserve to be treated with love and respect.

The truth is, we all deserve to be treated in this way, but, dear diva, it begins with how you treat yourself. It was Buddha (*Indian spiritual teacher and founder of Buddhism; 563–483 BC*) who said, 'You yourself, as much as anybody in the entire universe, deserve your love and affection.' And only when you know how to treat *yourself* properly can you begin to treat those around you with the love and respect they deserve. It's a cycle, and once the cycle is in motion, it is very difficult to stop its momentum.

## 2. Be prepared to learn and to develop yourself

Whether you are perfectly happy with who you are or would like to improve some aspect of your attitude or behaviour, be prepared to invest in yourself. One of the outstanding features of all successful divas is their lifelong commitment to developing themselves – mind, body and spirit. And when I talk about 'successful divas', I don't just mean successful businesswomen – I mean marvellous mothers and great homemakers too.

You don't necessarily need lots of money – finding a mentor is a very cost-effective way of growing your potential – but the time you need to invest *will* be expensive. Don't feel bad about taking time for you. Your family, children, friends, employers, employees and everyone else deserve to be in the presence of the best 'you' that you can be.

## 3. Take responsibility for your life

Stop with the blame. It doesn't matter who you think is to blame for what has gone wrong in your life – your parents, your teachers, your husband, your children, your bosses, your accidents or incidents, your bad luck, your lack of ability, your lack of time, your lack of money – there is only one common factor. What is it? The word 'your'.

This is *your* life, so you need to take responsibility for making it the best one possible. Stop demanding rights and accept full responsibility. Even if someone has broken into your house and stolen everything you own, take responsibility for your reaction. Even if your boss has fired you because you refused to yield to his irresistible charms (yuck), take responsibility for keeping your self-respect. If you have lost a limb in an accident that was no fault of your own, take responsibility for your rehabilitation. It is their ability to take responsibility for their lives that distinguishes the goddesses.

## 4. Don't let discrimination and inequality get the better of you

Whether you like it or not, whether you wish it away or ignore it, prejudice, discrimination and inequality exist. Of course everyone has a responsibility to fight this, starting with recognising our own prejudices and judgements, but we owe it to ourselves to rise above the inequalities of the world. Graça Machel said that it is only when women are treated fairly that we can talk of equality.

That is not going to happen in this lifetime, so we have to choose – to be victims of inequality, or to be divas who, regardless of the bigotry of others, make the most of ourselves and our situations. Let's rise above the ignorance of the people who want to keep us trapped in the box marked 'Children, Disabled People and Women'.

## 5. Stop *saying* and start *doing*

The New Age philosophers embrace the maxim 'the universe applauds action'. You can find similar sentiments in most holy texts. Fine, so let's start doing. But how? Saying, 'I will change my attitude' or 'I accept responsibility for my life' or 'I won't let any prejudiced bastards grind me down' is all well and good, but how does this translate into action?

It starts, strangely enough, with investing in yourself. Start reading more books, start having meaningful conversations with a variety of people and different groups, start talking to yourself in the mirror as if you are someone you adore, start embracing new skills, start learning how to do deals and start taking better care of yourself. All this leads back to self-respect. Weird how these cycles work, isn't it?

## 6. A little self-promotion goes a long way

As a rule, Americans are very good at self-promotion. They are comfortable telling you about their qualifications, accomplishments, successes and unique skills. The Indians (from the Indian subcontinent) are more modest, but when they introduce themselves to you in business, it is by name and qualification. The English are the polar opposite. It's like pulling teeth trying to get them to discuss their achievements. Even if you force the issue, they will sneak in a few self-deprecating comments.

Which of these groups describes you? As a woman, particularly in business, you have to work *much* harder than a man to establish your credentials – even if you are far more qualified than him. When I share a lecture podium with a man, even if he gives the barest minimum of an introduction, his authority is accepted. However, when I stand up, unless I firmly state my credentials upfront, I often find my knowledge unnecessarily challenged – by both the men *and* the women in the audience. The majority of the men have grey hair, which might be a factor, but I am not always younger than the male lecturers.

Do not be too modest in stating who you are and what you have achieved. Be proud of your achievements and, if you brag about them – and you should – be sure to include a few comments that are self-effacing to balance your bit of personal promotion. If you don't, can't or won't promote yourself, just who do you think is going to do it for you? Nobody, that's who, and you and your tremendous accomplishments will quickly be forgotten. Remember, always, that you have a story to tell.

If you are daunted by the prospect of all the changes that need to take place for your transformation from doormat to diva, fear not. I want to share an email with you that I received from someone who saw a transformation in herself in just two days. This note was written by Sharon 'Shaz' Maxwell, a sexy, sassy, confident woman with whom I work, who believed she had lost touch with her inner goddess. By simply being exposed to some of the amazing women who were interviewed for this book, Shaz 'found' herself once more. The same should happen for you.

> I really want to thank you for affording me the privilege of experiencing the last two days with you and meeting these most phenomenal women with whom you are connected. I can hardly believe the insight and strength of regaining myself I've had. When I lived in England in my thirties it was the happiest time of my life, and yet I didn't feel as fulfilled as I do now.
>
> Les [Shaz's husband] and I actually went out on a date tonight. He didn't know it was a date until I told him. We had the most delightful evening as I related the stories I'd heard over the last couple of days about these incredible women and their insights. What was most exciting was that it made me realise

we all have a story to tell. I suddenly realised that, when I'd felt so 'on the spot' at a recent training course, I actually had a story to tell that would have made me noticeable and memorable! Elizabeth [Malumo – her story is included later] might know how to strip and reassemble an FN rifle, but I've fired a 12-bore automatic Beretta in my stilettos! That story would have made the other people on the training course remember me – I just didn't think it was relevant!

My goodness, what a lot I've learnt in two short days! People are interested in true-life stories, but I just never thought mine were good enough because they didn't involve huge struggles and accomplishments. Les very kindly pointed out to me that after any business function we attend, his colleagues always ask after me and say, 'Your wife is so funny.' I feared it was the wine working its velvet influence on me, but now I see I have the same confidence in a work situation when sober.

What has struck me with the ladies we've interviewed is that they have risen far and beyond culture and colour, because they see the bigger picture. You are what you make of yourself. I realise that now.

By the way, Shaz is a member of a terribly exclusive four-diva *Thin Cows' Club*, which guzzles champagne and eats calorific lunches every month. A little group like this may sound silly, but start one of your own and see what happens. Letting your hair down with like-minded people who will support and not judge you is good for the soul.

You do need to make a conscious choice to be a diva, but, as Shaz points out, it really is up to you how you see yourself. As I said in *Work Diva*, if you are inclined to wallow in self-pity and the unfairness of life, you must adjust this attitude pronto. Divas are not victims, and they don't blame others – they count their blessings and have the world at their feet!

## WHEN WOMEN BECAME WORKERS

Before we go any further, I need to make an important point. I will talk a lot about the differences between men and women and, mostly, I'll encourage you to celebrate these differences. The days of the 'feminazi' (a marvellous term coined by American radio host Rush Limbaugh) are dead. Most women have realised that even though it is still a man's world, and that women do still suffer terrible prejudice and harm at the hands of men, it is our responsibility to charm, outwit and outmanoeuvre these men.

If you've ever heard the amazing Jenna Clifford talk – and we are privileged in this book to hear Jenna's views – she will tell you quite openly about the awful abuse she suffered personally, and about the abuse the planet is suffering because of the desire for power and the greed of men. Jenna, though, is quick to emphasise that not all men are bad – that there are wonderful, gentle, well-intentioned men with whom we can work to change the lot and, more importantly, the role, of women in the world.

Now, while contemplating the good, the bad and the gorgeous men in our world, let's have a laugh at the ignorance of the fellows who weren't lucky enough to be exposed to divine divas in their day.

The following is an extract from the July 1943 issue of *Transportation Magazine*. This was written for male supervisors of women in the workforce during World War II. How much has really changed?

Guide to Hiring Women

There's no longer any question whether transit companies should hire women for jobs formerly held by men. The draft and manpower shortage has settled that point. The important things now are to select the most efficient women available and how to use them to the best advantage.

Here are eleven helpful tips on the subject from Western Properties:

1. Pick young married women. They usually have more of a sense of responsibility than their unmarried sisters, they're less likely to be flirtatious, they need the work or they wouldn't be doing it, they still have the pep and interest to work hard and to deal with the public efficiently.

2. When you have to use older women, try to get ones who have worked outside the home at some time in their lives. Older women who have never contacted the public have a hard time adapting themselves and are inclined to be cantankerous and fussy. It's always well to impress upon older women the importance of friendliness and courtesy.
3. General experience indicates that 'husky' girls – those who are just a little on the heavy side – are more even-tempered and efficient than their underweight sisters.
4. Retain a physician to give each woman you hire a special physical examination – one covering female conditions. This step not only protects the property against the possibilities of lawsuits, but reveals whether the employee-to-be has any female weaknesses which would make her mentally or physically unfit for the job.
5. Stress at the outset the importance of time and the fact that a minute or two lost here and there makes serious inroads on schedules. Until this point is gotten across, service is likely to be slowed up.
6. Give the female employees a definite daylong schedule of duties so that they'll keep busy without bothering the management for instructions every few minutes. Numerous properties say that women make excellent workers when they have their jobs cut out for them, but that they lack initiative in finding work themselves.
7. Whenever possible, let the inside employee change from one job to another at some time during the day. Women are inclined to be less nervous and happier with change.
8. Give every girl an adequate number of rest periods during the day. You have to make some allowances for feminine psychology. A girl has more confidence and is more efficient if she can keep her hair tidied, apply fresh lipstick and wash her hands several times a day.
9. Be tactful when issuing instructions or in making criticisms. Women are often sensitive; they can't shrug off harsh words the way men do. Never ridicule a woman – it breaks her spirit and cuts off her efficiency.

DEAL *Diva*

10. Be reasonably considerate about using strong language around women. Even though a girl's husband or father may swear vociferously, she'll grow to dislike a place of business where she hears too much of this.
11. Get enough size variety in operators' uniforms so that each girl can have a proper fit. This point can't be stressed too much in keeping women happy.

# Chapter 2

## DIVAS GET WHAT THEY DESERVE

> 'Women who set a low value on themselves make life hard for all women.'
> – *Nellie McClung (Canadian feminist, politician and activist; 1873–1951)*

Let's start by challenging the statement made by the title of this chapter. Are women getting what they deserve? If you think this is *true*, you might think that women get the same salaries and promotion opportunities as men, or that women who choose to sacrifice their careers and raise the children are rewarded appropriately. Perhaps you think that the world is not unfair and that everyone gets what they deserve. Yeah, right, carry on smoking those socks!

If you think the statement is *untrue*, I'm right there with you, sister. But in that case, dare we ask who is to blame? Is it the doormat mentality? Or inequality in an unjust world? Perhaps the female inclination to avoid conflict? Or is it women's lack of skills to negotiate what they want?

Did you know that research shows women earn on average about 25 per cent less than their male counterparts for doing the same job? Or that the starting salaries of male graduates are nearly 10 per cent higher than that of female graduates? These statistics are all true and based on the findings of Linda Babcock and Sara Laschever for their book *Women Don't Ask: Negotiation and the Gender Divide*.

Here is some more information – or 'surprising facts', as the authors call them – extracted from their book. Although this study was conducted in the USA in the early 2000s, current global trends are in line with these stats.

Women Don't Like to Negotiate
- Two and a half times more women than men said they feel 'a great deal of apprehension' about negotiating.
- Men initiate negotiations about four times more often than women.
- When asked to pick metaphors for negotiations, men picked 'winning a ballgame' and a 'wrestling match', while women picked 'going to the dentist'.
- Women are more pessimistic about the rewards available, and so come away with less when they do negotiate – on average 30% less than men.
- Twenty per cent of women say they never negotiate at all, even though they recognise negotiation as appropriate and even necessary.

Women Suffer when they Don't Negotiate
- By not negotiating a first salary, an individual stands to lose more than $500,000 by age 60 – and men are more than four times more likely than women to negotiate a first salary.
- Starting salaries for men graduating from Carnegie Mellon were 7.6% higher than for women – and through negotiation, the men were able to improve their starting salaries by 7.4%, or about $4,000.
- In 2001 in the US, only 10.9% of the board of directors' seats at Fortune 1,000 companies were held by women.
- Women own about 40% of all businesses in the US but receive only 2.3% of the available equity capital needed for growth.

Women Have Lower Expectations and Lack Knowledge of their Worth
- Many people are so happy with a job offer that they fail to negotiate their salary.
- Women don't know their market value: women reported salary expectations between 3 and 32% lower than those of men for the same job; men expect to

earn 13% more during their first year of full-time work and 32% more at their career peak.

Recent research suggests that, if anything, the situation for women may have worsened. A 2004 report showed that women's wages in the USA amounted to only 76.5 per cent of men's wages (as opposed to the 76.8 per cent found by Babcock and Laschever in 2001) – a deterioration rather than an improvement (source: www.allexperts.com). This finding was corroborated by the Institute for Women's Policy Research, which revealed that the workplace pay gap between men and women, once thought to be narrowing, has, in fact, been moving in the opposite direction.

The following table (edited), prepared by the Statistics Division of the United Nations Secretariat from the International Labour Office, *Yearbook of Labour Statistics 2003* (accessed 2005), shows the extent of this problem on a global scale.

| STATISTICS AND INDICATORS ON WOMEN AND MEN WOMEN'S WAGES RELATIVE TO MEN'S |||
| --- | --- | --- |
| Country | Year | Women's wages in manufacturing as a percentage of men's wages |
| **Africa** | | |
| Botswana | 2003 | 52 |
| Egypt | 2002 | 68 |
| Kenya | 1997 | 123 |
| Swaziland | 1997 | 63 |
| **America, North** | | |
| Costa Rica | 2001 | 83 |
| Mexico | 2001 | 70 |
| Panama | 1999 | 93 |

DEAL *Diva*

| STATISTICS AND INDICATORS ON WOMEN AND MEN WOMEN'S WAGES RELATIVE TO MEN'S |||
|---|---|---|
| Country | Year | Women's wages in manufacturing as a percentage of men's wages |
| **America, South** | | |
| Brazil | 2002 | 61 |
| Colombia | 2003 | 65 |
| Peru | 1995 | 55 |
| **Asia** | | |
| Bahrain | 2002 | 44 |
| Hong Kong SAR | 2002 | 64 |
| Iran (Islamic Republic of) | 2001 | 80 |
| Japan | 2003 | 60 |
| Jordan | 2001 | 65 |
| Mongolia | 2003 | 87 |
| Myanmar | 1999 | 112 |
| Philippines | 1998 | 80 |
| Qatar | 2001 | 194 |
| Republic of Korea | 2002 | 56 |
| Singapore | 2003 | 61 |
| Sri Lanka | 2003 | 81 |
| Thailand | 2001 | 72 |
| Turkey | 1997 | 97 |
| **Europe** | | |
| Austria | 2001 | 60 |
| Denmark | 2002 | 87 |
| France | 2002 | 78 |
| Germany | 2003 | 74 |
| Greece | 1998 | 82 |

| STATISTICS AND INDICATORS ON WOMEN AND MEN WOMEN'S WAGES RELATIVE TO MEN'S |||
|---|---|---|
| Country | Year | Women's wages in manufacturing as a percentage of men's wages |
| Hungary | 2002 | 74 |
| Netherlands | 2000 | 78 |
| Portugal | 1999 | 64 |
| Sweden | 2003 | 91 |
| Switzerland | 2002 | 133 |
| Ukraine | 2003 | 69 |
| United Kingdom | 2003 | 79 |
| **Oceania** Australia | 2002 | 89 |
| New Zealand | 2003 | 80 |

Extracted from:
http://unstats.un.org/unsd/demographic/products/indwm/ww2005/tab5g.htm
Visit the website for the full table.

According to an analysis conducted by the Centre for Economic Performance (CEP) at the London School of Economics in July 2006, it would take 150 years for the income gap between the two genders to close in Britain (source: www.expressindia.com).

**South Africa**
What about South Africa, which, I noted with interest, was not included in the United Nations Statistics Division report? Well, it's not a happy picture either.
- Since the inception of the Businesswomen's Association's (BWA) 'Women in Corporate Leadership Census' in 2004, the percentage of female executive

management has increased from 14.7 per cent to 25.3 per cent (in real numbers, this is an increase from 739 to 1 227 women) (source: *BWA Magazine*, summer 2008).
- Statistics South Africa's figures show, however, that the number of women in management positions dropped from 2007 to 2009.
- A whopping 39.6 per cent of Johannesburg Stock Exchange (JSE)–listed companies have zero (none, not one, niks, nada, nothing) female directors (source: *BWA Magazine*, summer 2008).
- The socioeconomic level of women has dropped from 2007 (95.8 for women:100 for men) to 2009 (85.7:100) (source: Mastercard Worldwide Index of Women's Advancement, July 2009).
- An article in the January 2010 edition of *Fairlady* magazine cited a pay gap between men and women in South Africa of around 25 per cent. This mimics the disparity of the United States, Germany, France and any number of other countries.
- Some good news – provisional registrations for 2010 at the University of South Africa (UNISA) showed that 59.74 per cent of applicants were women and 40.26 per cent were men (source: Professor George Subotzky, UNISA).

In an article published in *Convergence* magazine (Vol. 8, No. 1), titled 'Why They Leave: Reasons Executive Women Flee South African Organisations', Desray Clark had this to say about the state of women in business:

> ABSTRACT: South African corporations appear unable to retain senior women, even though the retention of women executives produces long-term competitive advantage and improved company performance. Evidence suggests women's voluntary turnover rates are increasing when compared with those of their male counterparts. In South Africa this situation is intensified and the average voluntary turnover rate of local women executives is 17.15% – three times the rate of their male counterparts (Republic of South Africa, *Employment Equity Report*, 2004).

ARTICLE: Almost three-quarters of respondents felt that their ability to make a difference was hampered by their own lack of political acumen and negotiation ability.

> 'I should really have been more politically astute instead of being so open and honest. I am just naïve, I guess.' (respondent)
>
> 'My pride really wouldn't let me stay <when> another person at the same level as me told me about his perks and his salary; and they were twice as much as mine. That's when I decided: bugger you all!' (respondent)

Organisations are failing to keep their female talent because of their paternalistic organisational culture, the poor quality of management and their inability to accommodate top female performers, even though they have relatively few requirements.

Enough facts and figures to convince you that women are getting a lousy deal?

## WHY ARE WOMEN GETTING A DODGY DEAL?

If Linda Babcock and Sara Laschever are to be believed, one of the reasons women get a raw deal is because they can't, or *won't*, negotiate. Which brings us back to the subject of negotiation.

By now you are either wondering why we are talking about negotiation when this book is called *Deal Diva*, or you have figured out that negotiation is a critical element in dealmaking. If you can't negotiate, you are not able to close the best possible deals. We will get stuck into these concepts a bit later, so don't stress if you're worried that with what you have learnt so far, you're going to be a half-baked deal diva. By the end of this book you will definitely be a divine and complete cake, but, in the meanwhile, let's think about negotiation and dealmaking as one concept.

When I started doing research for this book, I was already absolutely convinced that women do not get the same deals as men – either in business or in life – and was pretty sure that the reason for this was because they aren't as good at negotiating as men. These views were based on my experience working with women while I created The Dealdiva™ programme for my organisation. Dealdiva™ is a course for 'women only' that focuses on helping them improve their dealmaking skills, particularly their ability to negotiate and close deals.

As I interviewed the fabulous females for this book, though, I noticed four patterns emerging that were somewhat at odds with the theories of Linda Babcock and Sara Laschever:

1. *Successful* women – whether businesspeople or homemakers – *do* know how to negotiate.
2. Women who lack confidence or experience are usually poor negotiators.
3. Women with a victim or doormat mentality – a mindset of scarcity rather than abundance – are routinely the worst negotiators.
4. Women value themselves differently from men.

This last point was a revelation to me. Sure, I've always been aware that what women consider to be valuable is different from what men consider to be valuable (just listen to the lyrics of Steely Dan's song 'Reelin' in the Years'), but I had no idea of the *extent* of the difference.

## VALUE, NEGOTIATION AND PROSTITUTION

In the olden days, people used to talk about 'win-win'. You probably remember the expression. In simple terms, it meant that, when a deal was done, both sides were happy with what they'd got. The counter to win-win was 'win-lose', where only one party or person came away from a transaction with what they wanted. 'Lose-lose' was when nobody was happy with the deal. Why the past tense for 'win-win'? Because it's so yesterday! Now it's all about 'value'.

Negotiation is as old as the oldest profession, which, as you know, is prostitution. The negotiation element was (and still is) the amount the woman received for whatever services she provided. Half a dozen hens' eggs for a bit of foreplay, perhaps? If my father is to be believed, this is how my maternal grandfather met his end – he was allegedly shot dead in a Glasgow pub arguing about the price of a prostitute. Then again, my father also told me that Ann-Margret (*Swedish-American actress, singer and dancer; 1941–*) was his sister – a story I proudly repeated to one of my primary-school teachers.

Back to the general history of negotiation (rather than my dubious heritage): the early theories of business negotiation, as we know it today, were formulated in the first half of the 20th century and generally espoused win-lose outcomes – for one party to achieve success, the other party had to be beaten. In the 1970s, the approach to negotiation started to change. Based largely on the industrial-relations events of the time, it was suggested that win-lose was fine for short-term goals, but win-win – or happy-happy, as I prefer to call it – was needed to entrench longer-term relationships. By the 1980s, and into the 1990s, 'win-win' was the phrase *de jour*.

In today's world, dealmaking, selling and negotiation are all about value. In exchanging value for value, both sides automatically achieve happy-happy. The issue I have with win-win is that it's fairly intangible – a good salesperson, whether selling you a second-hand car or trying to get you to examine his 'etchings' – may make you feel happy at the time, but in the cold light of day, another look at the situation could change your mind. Value-value is sustainable and measurable and thus promotes long-term relationships, and yet some people still go on about win-win. Go figure.

That women have a more complex approach to value than men do suggests that they have a better understanding of the subject. Why, then, do they not get the same deals as men in business? Perhaps the first issue to understand is how women calculate value. Value for women works on three levels:

1. How we value ourselves at a very personal, individual level.
2. How we value ourselves for the work we do – in other words, what should we get paid?
3. How we calculate value as part of a bigger picture – for example, being able to work flexitime, having a crèche at the office or experiencing a pleasant work environment.

Let's deal with each one separately.

## HOW TO VALUE YOU
*How do we value ourselves at an individual level?*

If you are thinking, 'Aha, this is the diva versus the doormat conversation again,' you would be right, and it's a conversation we don't need to repeat. However.

Men generally have a lot more testosterone and a lot less self-doubt than women, which translates into greater self-confidence. In tangible, measurable terms, this means that they are able to march into their boss's office and ask for – and expect – an increase or promotion. Women are inclined to question whether they should ask and ponder the consequences of asking. They are concerned about whether or not the company can afford it, worry about what will happen if the boss says no, and so on and so on. And then they do nothing and 'settle' for whatever comes their way.

Linda Babcock and Sara Laschever assert that women may 'have lower expectations'. No self-respecting diva has 'lower expectations'! She lives by the words of Timothy Leary (*American psychologist, futurist and advocate of psychedelic drug research; 1920–1996*), who said, 'Women who seek to be equal with men lack ambition.' As women, we need to think less and ask for more – we are worth what we are worth! But how much is that exactly?

## HOW TO VALUE THE WORK THAT YOU DO
*How should we value ourselves for the work that we do?*

Babcock and Laschever found that 'women don't know their market value'. This is often true, and utterly unforgivable. It does not matter whether you are a businesswoman or a homemaker, you must know your value in quantitative terms – in numbers, in other words. There are typically two issues at play when women don't know their market value – an aversion to numbers and a lack of homework. Let's start with the numbers.

In *Work Diva* I write about women who say that they are no good with numbers. Nothing has changed. This is still one of the most common protestations I hear from women when I talk about calculating values, determining averages or interpreting statistics. As I've said before, I believe that this aversion to numbers stems from an outdated education system where boys were told that they were good with mathematics and the sciences, and girls were told that they were good with languages and creative subjects. Language and mathematics (linear reasoning) are both left-brain abilities, so if you are good with languages, it stands to reason that you must be good with maths too. It is a mental block, not a lack of ability, that stands in your way, and it's time to throw out this limiting nonsense and start talking numbers, girlfriend – money and value.

Now to homework: There are very few women I have met who are lazy. Women graft their bottoms off (although, when you hit forty, the fat clings to your ass like the proverbial leech). As Jane Sellman (*American professor and writer*) said, 'The phrase "working mother" is redundant.' Women work hard to prove themselves, they run around after their kids and they have to multitask (even though recent scientific evidence suggests that you lose ten IQ points when you multitask). They hold down demanding careers while looking like a million dollars, and they still do the cooking and cleaning too. I have, however, met quite a few bone-idle men who do the minimum possible to get ahead – or to help their women, for that matter. Yet these men are smart enough to keep high-powered jobs and earn plenty of money. How do they do it? They understand that *information is power*. But more on that later.

If women aren't too lazy to do their homework or obtain the information on how much they are worth, it can only be that they don't know *how* to determine their value in actual money terms.

## Working Girls

We're talking about women in employment here, not ladies of the night. You owe it to yourself, diva, to know exactly what you are worth and how much you should be earning. I was interviewed for a leading women's magazine recently and was asked some thought-provoking questions on how working women should determine their value and their salaries. Here are a few ideas prompted by that interview.

## 1. Determining your worth to an organisation

You are worth as much as someone is willing to pay you, just as a house is worth whatever someone will offer for it. You need to push the envelope – go for a few interviews and ask for a cheeky salary package with each position. In doing this, you will be able to establish what you are worth to an employer. Don't be asinine, though – it's no good expecting a director's salary if you are applying to be the secretary to a director.

Always remember the mirror – how *you* see your intrinsic worth is how an employer will see it too.

And don't forget that a little self-promotion goes a long way – practise what you will say in an interview. Stand in front of the mirror and wax lyrical about your qualifications, accomplishments, awards, successes and unique skills. Don't be shy – just do it!

## 2. Asking for the salary you want

Women can be their own worst enemies when it comes to asking for the salary (or the increase) they want. They are often so grateful to get the job that they are hesitant to demand the salary a man would simply expect. Only when women start to value their worth properly will they stop this nonsense of selling themselves short. Women *are* taken less seriously in business a lot of the time, which means that they also need to work harder than men to establish their credentials.

Once you have established your credibility, be brave enough to tell the prospective employer what you want – your working conditions, benefits and salary package. Many of the women I meet, whether in business or socially, lack assertiveness, and negotiation does require a little bravery. By the way, super-aggressive, ball-busting bitches also need to learn to be assertive. Assertiveness is essential in getting what you want.

## 3. Calculating your market value – in numbers

I was once approached by a headhunter to interview for the position of local CEO for a large global organisation. I did not want the position, but I thought it would be a good opportunity to test my value in the corporate market. I told the headhunter that I would go for the interview only if the employer was prepared to look at a salary package of R$x$ (I asked for a very specific amount of money – the most I could imaginably justify). The recruiter baulked, but the organisation was still keen to recruit me.

Try this out for yourself – it's the best way to determine your market value in exact numbers. Bear in mind that when the recruitment company asks what you are currently earning – and they *will* ask – communicate your detailed salary expectations, as well as your current salary (and don't fib!). If the recruitment company gives you a hard time about what you are asking for, take the opportunity to practise some self-promotion. It will be a good trial run for when you need to present this argument to the prospective employer.

### 4. Negotiating your salary in turbulent times

The point at which you have the most power to negotiate your salary package is when you join an organisation. Once you are an employee, the company (usually via human resources) will tell you that 'the company's policy this year is an increase of $x$ per cent, or 'the salary range for your position is $y$ to $z$, so we can't give you the raise you want'. Companies hide behind these statements in order to control their payroll expenses, which is what their shareholders expect of them.

It is a tug of war that the player with the most power wins. What is 'the most power'? If you really need your job and can't move companies for whatever reason, you lose. If you are an indispensable employee, you win. In recessionary times, companies want their 'dead wood' to move on, but they will pay a premium to keep the people they value. If you are indispensable, you don't have to 'settle'. People who are irreplaceable either work very hard or have a unique set of skills – and they tell their employers what they expect to earn as a reward for their contribution.

### 5. Working hard and hoping to be rewarded

Let's separate working hard and taking on extra work. You get paid a salary to deliver a certain job to a certain standard. A diva always does this to the best of her ability. A lot of the doormats I meet aren't prepared, for whatever excuses, to give of their best and then wonder why they don't get the big fat increases or promotions. There is, however, no reason to be a martyr – martyrs are recognised only after they're dead!

If you want to earn more by taking on additional responsibilities, you can either ask for added responsibility, or you can just assume the extra work and then tell your employer that this is what you have done. In either case, be sure to communicate clearly how much you expect to be compensated for your efforts. If you don't get suitably rewarded, it's probably time to change jobs. Hoping to get an increase is a bit like hoping to win the lottery. There is no substitute for asking for the specific salary you want.

## 6. Being the flogged horse

The reality of the times in which we live is that employers are expecting more from their employees than ever before. If you are not available on email and cellphone after hours, you are perceived to be less than committed. Companies are very good at espousing 'work–life balance', but few of them truly believe it. When last did you go on holiday and not do any work?

You must take responsibility for communicating how you feel about your workload and where you see the boundaries. Don't just whinge and complain – work hard *and* communicate clearly. Let's face it – the people who typically get the promotions and higher salaries are the ones who have gone the extra mile. I have always worked like a dog and it has always paid off in some way or another – not necessarily financially, but certainly in developing my skills, reputation, self-worth and value.

## 7. Understanding why your value is not recognised

Try to understand why you are not more highly valued. Is it a clash with your boss, or a less-than-useful human resources department? Is it the culture of the company? Do you need to update your skills? Have you been making an effort and working hard? Perhaps you've got a lousy value proposition for the product 'you'? Have you communicated properly what you see as your value?

If you do have an issue with a superior, discuss it with someone in the organisation who will be able to help. If you have a problem with your direct boss, going around them or over their head may be the only option – you have a bad relationship anyway, so try to do something constructive about the situation.

Keep in mind that you can't expect people to *guess* what you think you are worth – you must communicate (and be able to defend) your exact salary expectations. If you still can't get what you want, and you have done everything to fix this, give of your best until you find another position.

Unfortunately, people sometimes need to stay in jobs where they feel – or they actually are – taken advantage of or undervalued. Not letting the negative environment get you down while you look for something else is vital. This is easy for me to say, but in reality it is extremely hard to do. In his amazing book *Man's Search for Meaning*, Viktor Frankl deduces that the people who survived the concentration camps in World War II were those who could see a life beyond their current situation. While a bad job is hardly a concentration camp, it sure can feel like one. If you have no choice but to stay put in your current position, read *Man's Search for Meaning* and stick it out until you find the right position with the right company.

### Suzy Homemaker

On to the women who stay at home, work part time, raise families or become professional wives. *Don't skip this section if you are not a full-time homemaker. It may be the most important advice you ever get.*

A large number of women with full-time jobs are still expected to keep house, so whether or not you are a full-blown homebody, you need to be aware of the value you add in this context. In understanding your worth as custodian of the home, you can help your family to appreciate you more, which will hopefully prompt them to realise when they are taking you for granted. *Doormats* are taken for granted – they 'offer little resistance to ill-treatment' – and being taken for granted is allowing yourself to be used as a doormat!

Home-based women, just like working girls, need to work out how much it costs them to stay at home (or work part time), how much they are contributing *financially* to the household and how much they would be earning if they had not given up their careers. Your man might give you an allowance, or even free access to 'our' cash (in reality it is always 'his' cash), but it's not just about the money. So, as a homemaker, how can you calculate your value? You need to draw up a 'value balance sheet', and you do this by completing the following *five easy steps*.

## Step 1

You need to put a monetary value – in other words, an amount – in the table on the following page for each of the home services you provide. The best way to determine the amount is to work out how much you would have to pay someone to perform this task for you on a monthly basis – for example, animal care. I probably spend one whole day each month with my dogs – taking them to the vet, or feeding, training, washing and exercising them. I would expect to pay someone (with a car) about R250 per hour to do this on a contract basis. Thus R250 × 8 hours per month = a total of R2 000 per month.

If you don't know how much it would cost to pay for a service, find out! Do not include *any* of the expenses (in my dog example, exclude the petrol, shampoo, vet bills, etc.). If there are tasks you can think of that are not included in the list, add them to the blank spaces at the end. Exclude the amount for an item if you already pay someone else for that work (i.e. you don't do this work yourself).

The VALUE TOTAL (1) is what the breadwinner should pay you for your contribution to the home (the breadwinner, in this type of situation, effectively becomes the employer). To keep things simple, I have not factored tax into any of the calculations.

| VALUE OF HOMEMAKER'S WORK PER MONTH | AMOUNT |
|---|---|
| • Housework, or 'maid' | R |
| • Cooking, or 'chef' | R |
| • Gardening, or 'landscaper' | R |
| • Animal care, or 'pet nanny' | R |
| • Caring for sick family, or 'nurse' | R |
| • Child care, or 'nanny' | R |
| • Child supervision, or 'au pair' | R |
| • Child psychologist, or 'social worker' | R |
| • Child developer, or 'motivator or coach' | R |
| • Mom's taxi, or 'chauffeur' | R |
| • Home schooling, or 'teacher' | R |
| • Homework supervision, or 'tutor' | R |
| • School, extramural & sporting events, or 'coach' | R |
| • Helping with school events, or 'PTA representative' | R |
| • On-site maintenance supervision, or 'project manager' | R |
| • Supervising staff, or 'manager' | R |
| • Controlling and buying provisions for home (groceries, gifts, etc.), or 'stock controller' | R |
| • Accounts (recons, queries, paying bills), or 'bookkeeper' | R |
| • Calendar management, or 'time manager' | R |
| • Organising special occasions, or 'social planner' | R |
| • Travel services (internet research time, making bookings, coordinating travellers), or 'travel agent' | R |
| • Host for business functions at home, or *maitre d'hôtel* | R |

DEAL *Diva*

| VALUE OF HOMEMAKER'S WORK PER MONTH | AMOUNT |
|---|---|
| • Family obligations (e.g. tea with his mother), or 'caregiver' | R |
| • Pool cleaner, or 'yummy Latino' | R |
| • | R |
| • | R |
| • | R |
| • | R |
| • | R |
| VALUE TOTAL (1) | R |

## Step 2
Calculate how much money you currently receive each month – in the form of cash, credit card limits or allowances – from the breadwinner to perform the tasks you quantified in the table above. Do *not* include the money you are given for groceries, school fees, clothing, consumables or any other expenses – only write down what money you receive in exchange for providing these services.

| CASH TOTAL (2) | R |
|---|---|

## Step 3
Below, deduct the CASH TOTAL (2) from the VALUE TOTAL (1) to get the NET TOTAL (3). Fifty bucks says that your NET TOTAL (3) is a very large negative amount.

| VALUE TOTAL (1) | + R |
|---|---|
| CASH TOTAL (2) | – R |
| NET TOTAL (3) | = R |

## Step 4

You will have to do some personal research to get the information required for this step. You also need to include a monetary amount for any social or fringe benefits you would receive. If you don't know all of this information, go for a few interviews (with recruiters and companies) and find out! You can estimate this value in the meantime, but you will do yourself no favours if you don't get a real number for this step. Also, read *Outliers* by Malcolm Gladwell to comprehend fully how much value you lose when you stop working for any period.

| TOTAL SALARY PACKAGE | AMOUNT |
|---|---|
| • How much would you be earning now if you had continued working? | – R |
| • Multiply by number of years you have not worked | × |
| PACKAGE TOTAL (4) | = – R |

## Step 5

To extract all the worthwhile conclusions from this exercise, you should:

- Compare VALUE TOTAL (1) with PACKAGE TOTAL (4) to see how much it costs you financially to be the homemaker. If you have not been working for, say, five years, you can estimate the value of this over a five-year period.
- Add PACKAGE TOTAL (4) to NET TOTAL (3) to work out the real cost of your decision to be the homemaker, and then calculate over the period you have not worked.
- Use VALUE TOTAL (1) as the basis of what you should receive as income, *excluding* child support and any expenses, in the unfortunate event you were to get divorced. If you want to calculate a cash settlement amount, use PACKAGE TOTAL (4). For a list of the child support and other expenses you need to claim, get yourself a copy of *Beat the Bitch: How to Stop the Other Woman Stealing Your Man* by Tess Stimson. It is both an informative and riotous read.

This exercise is obviously not a perfect scientific study that produces irrefutable and completely accurate denominations, but as no such studies seem to exist, the amount you calculate is probably as good as any you will find. According to Liz Pulliam Weston (see http://moneycentral.msn.com/content/CollegeandFamily/P46800.asp for the full article), the statistics available on the real value of a homemaker are 'codswallop'. Liz goes on to say that, in the USA, 'The economic value of a stay-at-home spouse is closer to $30,000 a year. Our society doesn't place a high dollar value on a homemaker's work, and those who choose to stay home do so at their own economic peril.'

Is this true? Think of the women you know who have sacrificed their careers and their own interests to dedicate themselves to the lives of their families (whether by choice or circumstances). What do you think happens to these women if they get divorced or are widowed?

Another 'campaigner' for married and non-income-earning women is Tess Stimson. In her book *Beat the Bitch* (which I mention above), Tess talks about how to 'follow the money'. She says:

> You should always know what your man is earning, regardless of whether you think he might be cheating on you or not. Don't be a pathetic little woman who can't get her pretty head around numbers. Take some responsibility here.

A rich husband – whether you have one or are still looking for one – is no guarantee that you will be financially secure in the future. You might receive very little in a divorce settlement. A recent article on www.ioljobs.co.za stated that, contrary to popular belief, women – even if their husbands leave them for another woman – don't always get a house, a car and an income when the marriage ends. Tess Stimson supports this view. In *Beat the Bitch*, she points out:

> Statistically, men end up 25 per cent better off post-divorce than they were when they were married – principally because they're now keeping the lion's share of their income. Even if you're getting half, which is frankly unlikely,

you'll have to use it to support yourself and the kids. Which is why, on average, women end up 20 per cent worse off after a divorce.

In this day and age, women need to take responsibility for their financial lives. As Gloria Steinem (*American journalist, feminist and activist; 1934–*) said, 'Most women are one man away from welfare.'

Do you know what the 'Cinderella Complex' is? It's a common term in financial circles to describe women who have handed over their financial well-being to their husbands. The Cinderella Complex is the reason why so many women stay in dysfunctional relationships – they don't have the money, or the self-worth, to leave. It's also the reason certain women take no personal responsibility for their lives – they believe that they will be rescued by an outside force – whether it be Prince Charming, winning the lotto or marrying a billionaire.

Susan 'Suze' Lynn Orman (*American financial advisor and author; 1951–*), voted by *Time* magazine as one of the most influential people in the world – has written six bestselling books on the subject of personal finance for women. You owe it to yourself to buy at least one of her books to gain some insight into how you can become financially independent. Take responsibility for providing for yourself and your children, and *then* you can live happily ever after.

## VALUE AND THE BIGGER PICTURE

*How can we calculate value as part of a bigger picture – for example, being able to work flexitime, having a crèche at the office or enjoying a pleasant work environment?*

Earlier in this chapter I mentioned that women calculate their value very differently from men. Arrah Nielsen, a junior fellow with the Independent Women's Forum (a libertarian group in the USA), concluded in an article in 2005 that the pay gap between men and women disappears when other variables (type of job, hours worked in a week, tenure, maternity leave, etc.) are taken into account. Although I don't believe this to be entirely true, a woman's ability to look at the bigger picture can help to reduce pay disparity. Women place a high value on perks, such as receiving good maternity benefits, having a crèche at the office, being able to work flexible hours, reporting to a decent boss, enjoying a pleasant working environment, having easy access to schools and shops, and so on.

What is important, though, is that women appreciate the monetary value (or lack thereof) of these non-financial factors when calculating their total salary packages. A balance sheet similar to the one drawn up by Suzy Homemaker is necessary to accomplish this and is an integral part of preparing for a salary or promotion negotiation. Women should push for the same monetary component as men for the same job – and then be prepared to negotiate on cash versus benefits to ensure that they get the total remuneration package they want and deserve.

Don't be caught off guard or feel unsettled if the company throws the 'company policy' book at you in order to justify what you can and can't have when you are negotiating your salary package. Being flexible and including lots of different variables (I like to call them 'marbles') in your salary discussions is exactly what a skilled negotiator would do. As I've said, it does mean that you need to prepare for this type of conversation.

I once asked for an increase, and was told by the company's remuneration committee chairman that I was already the second-highest-paid woman on the African continent, so I couldn't expect a raise. I doubt if this was true, but I *was* earning a rather large salary. So instead of going for more money, I went after the extras like additional annual leave, an upgraded company car, a better office, a private secretary, a higher bonus percentage, paid subscriptions for magazines and clubs, and flights overseas (business class, of course!).

There are lots of benefits you could pursue as part of your salary negotiation. Here is a list of variables – or marbles – you can use in case you get stuck for ideas:
- Your job title.
- Job description or responsibilities.
- Define your own hiring and/or firing clauses (and other terms of engagement).
- A welcome bonus.
- Restraint of trade payment.
- Golden good-bye (termination payment).

- Performance bonuses.
- Different bonus to fixed-income split.
- Shares (or shares in lieu of salary or bonus).
- Profit-share.
- Provident or pension fund (contributory or not?).
- Contributory (or not) medical aid or hospital plan.
- Company pays your other long-term insurances.
- Company pays short-term insurance cover.
- Company car (or upgraded company car).
- Car allowance.
- All petrol and maintenance costs (or a petrol card).
- Business travel allowance and per diem.
- Flights overseas each year (business class or you can take a partner).
- Better or bigger office (or one on the executive floor).
- Therapeutic chair, or ergonomically designed keyboard, or pot plants.
- Parking close to the front door.
- Access to a secretary (or a private secretary).
- Choosing your own recruits (or defining your support team).
- Cellphone, PDA or laptop (or upgrades on the ones you have).
- Paid subscriptions for magazines and club memberships.
- Paid cellphone and internet bills.
- Extended leave (unpaid, sabbatical, maternity, annual, family, etc.).
- Flexible working hours.
- A longer (or shorter) lunch break.
- Working from home (or choosing where you are based).
- Relocation assistance or allowance.
- Training or mentoring programmes.
- Study leave.
- Company pays for your studies.
- Bringing your child (or pet) to work.
- Company pays crèche or child-care fees.

DEAL *Diva*

When you look at the bigger picture to calculate your value, don't be afraid to get down and dirty with the detail. For every single big picture, you will need lots and lots of marbles to give you the room to manoeuvre without compromising the total value of the package. And you, dear diva, deserve more than to 'compromise'.

## ONE FLAW IN WOMEN

*Women have strengths that amaze men.*
*They bear hardships and they carry burdens,*
*but they hold happiness, love and joy.*
*They smile when they want to scream.*
*They sing when they want to cry.*
*They cry when they are happy*
*and laugh when they are nervous.*
*They fight for what they believe in.*
*They stand up to injustice.*
*They don't take 'no' for an answer*
*when they believe there is a better solution.*
*They go without so their family can have.*
*They go to the doctor with a frightened friend.*
*They love unconditionally.*
*They cry when their children excel*
*and cheer when their friends get awards.*
*They are happy when they hear about*
*a birth or a wedding.*
*Their hearts break when a friend dies.*
*They grieve at the loss of a family member,*
*yet they are strong when they*
*think there is no strength left.*
*They know that a hug and a kiss*
*can heal a broken heart.*

*Women come in all shapes, sizes and colours.*
*They'll drive, fly, walk, run or email you*
*to show how much they care about you.*
*The heart of a woman is what*
*makes the world keep turning.*
*They bring joy, hope and love.*
*They have compassion and ideas.*
*They give moral support to their*
*family and friends.*
*Women have vital things to say*
*and everything to give.*

HOWEVER, IF THERE IS ONE FLAW IN WOMEN,
IT IS THAT THEY FORGET THEIR WORTH.

Author unknown

## Chapter 3

## FROM DIVA TO DEAL DIVA

'The minute you settle for less than you deserve, you get even less than you settled for.' – *Maureen Dowd*
*(American Pulitzer Prize–winning columnist; 1954–)*

When a woman – or anyone, for that matter – sets out to get what she wants, she presumably has a plan. She has probably thought through the approach that she is going to take, prepared all the arguments and counter-arguments, practised the conversations in her head, and she is now ready. Sound about right? Ironically, this is as much planning as most people will do – for some of the most important discussions of their lives! No self-respecting dealmaker or negotiator will invest so little time in preparing. The experts even prepare what they need to prepare!

The skilled dealmaker figures out the strategies that she will use to get what she wants, who will be in her team (and on the other party's side), what information she needs to obtain, her opening position and bottom line, the key issues and priorities, where she can be flexible and what she will want in return for being flexible, tactics for the face-to-face encounter (including whether or not to take a hard line), who will make the first move, how she is going to close down the deal – and let's not forget the implementation plan.

Scary? It's not as bad as it seems at first glance. There's an old adage that goes:

'How do you eat an elephant?' The answer is: 'In small bites.' We're going to work through all these issues in small bites so that, by the end of the book, you, too, will be negotiating like an expert.

## LESSONS FROM CHILDREN IN DEALMAKING

In the movie *The Sound of Music*, Maria (played by Julie Andrews) teaches the children to sing. She commences her music lesson by singing, 'Let's start at the very beginning, a very good place to start.' I'll skip the singing if you don't mind, but the very beginning is indeed the very best place to start. And we're going to begin with distinguishing between dealmaking and negotiation and selling – words that up till now have been used interchangeably.

Before you read any further, Google or consult a dictionary for a definition of the word 'deal' or 'dealmaker'. Find anything useful? Probably not. The website www.thefreedictionary.com defines a 'dealmaker' as 'one that makes deals, as in business, finance or politics'. The definition of 'deal' is: '1. to give out as a share or portion, apportion; 2. to distribute among several recipients; 3. sell' etc. Do you think that Sir Richard Branson or Donald Trump would agree with these definitions? They would laugh at them!

When I was creating The Dealmaker™ programmes for my company, I spent a lot of time researching the collective qualities that characterise the world's leading dealmakers. Based on my findings, I created a new definition for a dealmaker:

> A person skilled in using instinct, processes and expertise in primarily negotiation, selling and communication, and able to leverage or adjust the balance of power to bring closure to transactions that usually benefit all parties.
>
> © The Dealmaker Programmes Company

We will eat this definition in small bites. Let's start with the word 'instinct'. It may have surprised you a little to see this word. I got the idea from Donald Trump (*American business entrepreneur; 1946–*), who said, 'Dealmaking is not about being brilliant – it does take a certain intelligence – but mostly it's about instinct.'

From what I have seen, watching and working with some exceptional dealmakers, these business gurus rely as much on their instinct and intuition as they do on their ability to persuade, negotiate or communicate.

Back to basic instinct and an opinion I hold firm – we are all *born* with superb dealmaking skills. In the Introduction I made the statement that *'Deal Diva* is about putting the power back (yes, *back*) in your hands' – and it is. You need to reclaim the power with which you were born, dear diva. Dealmakers are not built – it's inborn! Just ask The Donald. How can I be so certain of this? The answer lies with children.

Cast your mind back to when you were a child and wanted a treat – maybe you wanted to be taken to the park, eat sweets before dinner or have your dog sleep in your bed. How did you get what you wanted? No doubt you used to beg, as in Jeremy Taylor's immortal (now immoral?) song lyrics 'Ag please daddy won't you take us to the drive-in?' This is known, in adult speak, as persuasion or selling – or begging, pleading or manipulating!

Children peak as dealmakers between the ages of five and eight. If you have kids in this age group, you will know exactly what I'm talking about. Try getting a six-year-old to go to bed if this is not what he wants to do. He will think up a whole range of reasons why he needs to stay up, or he might simply beg for five more minutes. Alternatively, he will ask for a vast variety of treats in exchange for going to bed – things like, 'If you take me to the lion park tomorrow', or, 'If my dog can sleep with me, then I'll go to bed now.' How do adults deal with these keen young minds? They say, 'Go to bed now *or else*' – or *'because I said so'*. Is this the best a grown-up can do? Unfortunately, it usually is. Why is it that a child, whose cognitive development is not yet complete, can often outmanoeuvre an adult? They are born negotiators.

Children make brilliant dealmakers because:
1. They tell you what they want: they live by the old saying, 'If you don't ask, you don't get.'
2. They are infinitely creative: they have lots and lots of ideas and alternatives – their marbles – with which to play.

3. They are infinitely flexible: they are willing to offer alternatives if they get a 'no'.
4. They do not apply associative logic to getting what they want: they will happily link bedtime with the lion park, bathing to ice cream, or being quiet with not eating vegetables.
5. They are ruthless little traders: they continually push their luck.
6. They don't care about ego and 'losing face': if you say 'no', they simply try again.

Funny thing this, but I see these same qualities in the world's leading dealmakers.

A couple of years ago I read *Freakonomics: A Rogue Economist Explores the Hidden Side of Everything* by Steven D Levitt and Stephen J Dubner. If you have not yet read the book, do yourself a favour and buy a copy. This is not your typical boring business book (if you're not convinced, just look at the front cover and then read the blurb on the back). In *Freakonomics*, the statement is made that 'Incentives are the cornerstones of modern life.' The authors go on to say: 'The typical economist believes the world has not yet invented a problem that he cannot fix if given a free hand to design the proper incentive scheme.'

Despite the recent crash in the global economy, this statement still holds true – incentives, ironically, are how governments are trying to fix the banking crisis. Maybe if the incentive schemes hadn't been so excessive in the first place... Anyhow, the authors – one of whom is a Harvard graduate who has won an award for being the best American economist under the age of forty – talk about how well children understand incentives. Children hold adults in the palms of their grubby little hands.

In my 'bedtime' example, the little boy understands that Mom wants something – for him to go to bed – and he instinctively uses this opportunity to try to get something for himself: an incentive (or carrot) of sorts. The boy also knows that Mom has more power than he does, but he still takes the gap. Why? Because this is how dealmakers operate. They recognise that with unlimited creativity and infinite flexibility, with no strict dependence on the rules, and with a persistent mentality of trading, they can usually get exactly what they want.

So we are all born with dealmaking abilities, but why, and when, do we lose them? If you have observed children (or if you can think back that far!) you will have noticed that most youngsters relinquish their persistent negotiating during primary school. In order for children to adapt to the rigours of school life, and because of their initial natural willingness to please and listen to their teachers, they start to conform to 'the system'. And when they unwittingly buy into the system, they lose their inherent trading skills – they stop expecting to get something in return for giving the other person what he or she wants. By the time they meet the next real 'system', commonly called 'business', their dealmaking abilities are long gone.

A few children don't lose their skills. They keep developing them, and they later emerge as outstanding dealmakers. Here is how it works: Imagine that you were born with a talent for tennis. You were really good when you were a kid, and you played tennis every day until you were nine. Then, for some reason, you didn't play tennis for ten years – how good would you be compared to the kids who had continued to play tennis? We know that all the great tennis players or golfers, for example, were coached continuously throughout their childhoods. It's the same for dealmakers. A few people don't lose their talent for negotiating, and when they reach the business world these individuals are streets ahead of everyone else.

Fear not, as there is still hope for you if you recognise that, along with your desire to stick your tongue out at boys, you lost your dealmaking skills. You are about to relearn them.

## SELLING, PERSUADING AND PLEADING

Now for the next bite of the elephant-sized definition: '*A person skilled ... in primarily negotiation, selling and communication*'. Most women are first-class communicators, but the plan is to take you from first class to friggin' awesome. However, let's put this aside for the moment.

Do you know that over half of the people I tested when I was developing The Dealmaker™ programmes could not clearly articulate the key differences between 'negotiating' and 'selling'? This is particularly concerning when you think of the number of customers who ask for discounts at the close of a sale. You don't have to hold a sales position to appreciate what I'm saying here – think about when *you* are the one asking for the discount. In order to handle these situations with aplomb, you need to understand the fundamental differences between selling and negotiating. Let's focus on 'selling' for the moment.

*Encarta Concise English Dictionary* describes 'selling' as 'the activity or process of persuading people to buy a product or service'. Hmmm. That doesn't really say much, does it? Their definition of 'persuade' is 'to successfully urge someone to perform a particular action, especially by reasoning, pleading or coaxing' – which is the punchline of a rather rude joke! If you work in sales or are exposed to salespeople, you will know that this is laughable. It's not fair to laugh, though, if you have no better suggestions to offer. Here's the one I came up with for The Dealmaker™ programmes:

> Activity or process of persuading another party to accept a specific deal, overcoming differences in objectives and/or viewpoints.
>
> © The Dealmaker Programmes Company

If you are thinking, 'Well, I'm not a salesperson, so all this stuff about selling doesn't apply to me,' wakey, wakey! To be a dealmaker of note, to get what you want, you *must* be able to sell – to persuade or to convince. It's as important in your skills set as mascara is in your make-up bag.

And if you are about to whinge that you don't know how to sell, that you've never had sales training … *stop*! If you could not sell, you would never have got a fraction of what you have in your life – jobs, dates, friends … These things didn't just drop from the sky. To get jobs, make friends and find lovers, *we sell ourselves*. We convince the party with whom we want the relationship – be it formal (such as employment, marriage, memberships, etc.) or informal (friendships, dating, book clubs and so on) – that we have something to offer.

Does this make you think that selling is a bit like being a prostitute? You got it, babe. Whether you are promoting (i.e. *selling*) your wonderful skills, your unique expertise, your charming companionship or your beautiful body, you are selling yourself. And, yes, that is what prossies do. They are a lot more honest than most other women in their transactions – they say upfront that they want the cash, whereas we would never say that we expect to be taken to a fancy dinner, preferably in France. Dame Rebecca West (*British author and travel writer; 1892–1983*) understood that at least hookers aren't doormats, as evidenced in *Mr Chesterton in Hysterics: A Study in Prejudice*, where she says, 'I only know that people call me a feminist whenever I express sentiments that differentiate me from a doormat or a prostitute.'

Selling is fun. Selling is easy. Selling allows you to persuade someone to give you what you want without you having to make sacrifices or give them something in return (not at all the case with negotiation). When you sell effectively, you get what you want. Period.

If you have ever been lucky enough to participate in any sales training, you will no doubt have been taught to 'overcome objections'. This is Sales 101. From real life, though, you will have learnt that selling doesn't always work. When a person's viewpoint is driven by strong emotion, it is very difficult to convince him or her to do what you want them to do, regardless of whether or not you present a brilliant value proposition. Emotion in any situation can make people behave irrationally.

Think about the Israeli–Palestinian conflict. What chance would you have of convincing the Israelis to accept that they have no right to the occupied territories? It just ain't gonna happen. How about persuading the Palestinians that this is not their homeland? Ditto. With emotional conflict of this magnitude, even a silvery-tongued salesman like Bill Clinton is unlikely to come away with a deal.

## NEGOTIATING, HORSE-TRADING AND COMPROMISING POSITIONS

If selling won't work, what other options are available to get someone to accept a deal, high emotion or not? There are quite a few alternatives, but let's stick with analysing our 'dealmaker' definition for the moment.

Along with selling, the other skill an expert dealmaker has is that of 'negotiation', which *Encarta* describes as 'resolving of disagreements; the reaching of agreement through discussion and compromise'. Compromise? Are they kidding? Do you have any idea what 'compromise' means? Well, here it is, courtesy of *Encarta* again: 'agreement; settlement of a dispute in which two or more sides agree to accept less than they originally wanted'. No, and I mean *no*, negotiator worth her salt goes into a deal intending to accept less than she wanted.

Negotiators approach deals like kids – with lots and lots of variables (marbles, carrots, sticks, incentives or concessions – call them what you will) in their back pockets. If part of their proposal is rejected, they pull out a new option. This is exactly what I recommended you do when you negotiate your salary package. If the company is not prepared to give you the salary for which you are asking, then take as much cash as you can get and supplement the package with different types of leave, an upgraded car, shorter working hours, a different split of fixed cash to bonus, you name it – until you get to the value that you originally wanted. It's not rocket science – your average six-year-old understands it!

As you can see, I feel rather passionately about fool negotiators who go into meetings to 'compromise'. They're not negotiators; they are wimps! Can you imagine Sir Richard Branson (*British industrialist; born 18 July 1950 – same day as Madiba!*) starting his meeting by saying, 'Okay, guys, nobody is leaving here with what they want.' No. He says, 'Screw it, let's do it.'

In the spirit of laughing, but offering an alternative, here is a definition of 'negotiation' that I believe works:

Process of reaching a deal acceptable to all parties, accommodating differences in objectives and/or viewpoints, through trading.

© The Dealmaker Programmes Company

Having had my little rant, let's go back to the Israeli–Palestine conflict and pretend we can send Sir Richard to negotiate the road-map deal that George W. Bush (*American president; 1946–*) failed to close. Sir Richard would, in all likelihood, say, 'Okay, guys, let's accept that you Palestinians detest the Israelis, and that you

Israelis despise the Palestinians. Are we agreed on that? Good, let's move forward. Now, Israel, what are the conditions under which you will do $x$?' ($X$ might be to withdraw from the Gaza Strip.)

After posturing and posing, the Israeli negotiators might say, 'If the Palestinians stop shelling us and we receive no reports of shelling for one year, then we will release $y$ section of the territory.' The Palestinians, after expressing suitable outrage, could say that they need time for Hamas and Fatah and the other political parties to agree this between themselves, but that in the meantime Israel should allow all aid through to Gaza, regardless from where it has been sent. And on and on it will go, like a tango (albeit with two very reluctant partners), backwards and forwards.

You might be tempted to see this as 'horse-trading', and you wouldn't be wrong, although 'trading' is the term negotiators prefer – calling them 'horse-traders' is somewhat like calling psychologists 'shrinks'. What the two parties will be doing is *giving to get* – quid pro quo, negotiating, trading or, yes, even horse-trading.

Agreement in this, or any other, conflict is going to come from 'accommodating' the differences between the two parties, not 'overcoming' them – which means (if you look again at my definitions of 'sales' and 'negotiation') through trading and not persuading. These skills are, however, inextricably intertwined:

- A deal could begin with selling or negotiating, yet selling usually opens a deal and negotiating closes it.
- A competent dealmaker can move seamlessly between negotiating and selling and then backwards and forwards and backwards and forwards, and on and on – much like a professional dancer.
- The best negotiators are good salespeople, just as the most successful salespeople are good negotiators.
- Basically, selling is *persuading* the other party to accept a deal while *overcoming* objections and differences of opinion, whereas negotiation is reaching a deal through *trading* (giving to get) while *accommodating* different views and objectives.

## A CATALOGUE OF CHOICES

Earlier on I mentioned that there are quite a few options you could use to get what you want, and now that we have examined the two main ones – selling and negotiating – we can have a look at the other alternatives. We have not quite finished with selling and we are certainly not done with negotiating, so don't fret if you're not yet confident that you know *how* to do the stuff the experts make look so easy. You are still well on track to becoming a deal diva!

By now you will have realised that in order to get what you want, you will most often sell (persuade) or negotiate (trade). Trading can be a bit expensive, particularly when you are dealing with high-value or high-cost items, so you need to try other options before you rush in ready to negotiate. Would it not be convenient if you could have a sort of shopping list from which you could choose the best ways to get what you want?

Your wish is my command. Here are the most common of the choices:
- Sell (persuade).
- Argue (wear down).
- Negotiate (trade).
- Bribe or blackmail (*not recommended, dear diva*).
- Surrender (roll over).
- Conquer (dictate).
- Problem-solve or conflict-resolve.
- Compromise, haggle or settle for less.
- Postpone.
- Gamble (take a bet, flip a coin).
- Walk away (wash your hands).
- Deadlock.
- External options (e.g. arbitration, mediation, legal action).
- Neutral options (e.g. auction, tender).
- And many more…

The easiest way to illustrate how to choose from this list is by using an example.

We should move away from Israel and Palestine, just in case you have reverted to thinking that dealmaking only applies to negotiating big business deals, important global agreements, or starting and stopping wars. Let's work with a case that is a little closer to home.

Picture the scene: You have finally been given a promotion at work to executive head of marketing. It's your dream job, but you have had to make many sacrifices and work extremely hard to get the position. Your company is paying you an excellent salary and is promising you a seat on the board of directors if you achieve certain objectives. The problem is that, to meet these objectives, you will be required to travel, both locally and abroad, for at least a week every month for a few years. You have a husband, and a daughter in primary school. Your husband is very unhappy about you being away from home for what will amount to three months a year. Although you want to make the most of your career without compromising your family, you figure it is only for a couple of years and your career is important to you. And you love to travel. What are your options?

**Persuade**

You now know that if you can persuade someone to let you have what you want, you will usually not have to make any sacrifices or give any concessions. So, first prize would be to convince your husband that the travelling will benefit not only you, but him and your daughter as well. What could you say to him? Your arguments might range from the importance of following one's passion and the opportunity he is being given to spend quality time bonding with your daughter to the contribution your big salary will make to the general well-being of the family, and to your daughter's education in particular. Or that the travelling would satisfy your wanderlust and you will then stay at home more in the future. Will he buy your line of reasoning? Possibly.

You could also manipulate him by telling him that you want to achieve your job objectives so that he will be proud of you, or that if he really loves you, he will support your ambitions. Or maybe that he if stops you from pursuing your dreams, you may always feel a little bit resentful. Now, don't get all sanctimonious about manipulation – women are good at using manipulation to get what they want, whether you want to admit it or not!

Persuasion costs you time; it might take a while to convince him that the travelling is a positive. If you are running out of time or the situation is becoming emotional, you may want to try negotiating with him.

## Negotiate

Negotiation is about trading – about giving to get. What could you offer your husband in return for him supporting your travel? You may offer to: (1) Assist him financially if ever he wanted a sabbatical or a change of career. (2) Pay for him to play golf at St Andrews or for coaching from Tiger Woods's coach (okay, bad idea). (3) Have him and your daughter join you for one big overseas trip a year. (4) Help him by allowing your dreaded mother-in-law to move into your home. The list is endless, but you would probably try to offer him whatever it is that presses his 'hot buttons' – motorbike-racing in *my* man's case (and, yes, I have taken him to MotoGP at Donnington Park, armed with a VIP pass in his mitts). What could the cost of all of this be to you? You might be mortgaging your future happiness or your financial independence.

## Bribe or blackmail

By now you are probably thinking that negotiation sounds pretty similar to bribery – and you would be quite correct. There is only one difference between negotiation and bribery, and that is that the latter is generally seen in a negative light. According to the definitions of 'bribery', it is not necessarily illegal – it's about ethics: One man's bribery is another man's negotiation. The site www.thefreedictionary.com defines bribery as: '1. Something, such as money or a favour, offered or given to a person in a position of trust to influence that person's views or conduct; or 2. Something serving to influence or persuade.'

You would never stoop to bribery, right? Well, let me ask you: What do you offer your kids in exchange for eating their peas? Or someone at work to cover for you? Or your husband to take you out for dinner? Or your teenage son to clean the swimming pool? Incidentally, teenagers respond *very* well to bribery. And did you realise that bribing your children to eat their fruit and vegetables is good practice? An article released by Tesco PLC in July 2001 suggests that offering incentives (literal carrots!) to your kids to eat their greens should lead to healthy long-term eating patterns. And you felt guilty about secretly offering bribes for a clean plate?

At what point does negotiation become bribery? You need to draw your line in the sand based on your own value system, but I use the following delineation: If offering somebody something in exchange for getting what I want is going to lead to trouble with the law, my family or friends, my customers or colleagues, it is probably the wrong side of negotiation.

Blackmail is a form of negotiation that contains a threat or *dis*incentive (a stick or a rotten carrot). If someone doesn't do *x* for you, then *y* will happen to them. It is similar to bribery, but the upside for the other person is avoiding an unpleasant outcome rather than receiving an incentive or a carrot. For example, if your teenager does not keep her room tidy, she won't get her allowance or get to use the car that week.

A proposal containing a disincentive is never first prize as it can seriously harm a relationship. As with the ethical versus moral line on where blackmail would become illegal, if in doubt, steer absolutely clear.

**Surrender**

Back to the 'promotion but must travel' example. Another option, of course, would be to just accept your husband's position: simply roll over and don't travel, or find a new job. This obviously has a price, too. What will the cost of surrendering be to your future happiness? Your career prospects? Your financial well-being? Will you ever get your own way with your husband again? Will he respect you for simply giving in and showing no perseverance or backbone? Are you being a good role model for your daughter? Albeit not measurable, the penalties in this option are potentially massive. Is this a better option than negotiating with your hubby? Your call. Surrender certainly wouldn't be my choice.

## Conquer

The opposite option to surrendering would be to defy your husband and do what *you* want to do, whether he likes it or not. You may be able to approach another family member, perhaps your mother or an aunt with whom you have a good relationship, to look after your daughter when you are away. Alternatively, you could hire an au pair, or move your sister into the house to care for your daughter (she won't touch your man, will she?).

Taking the 'conquer' route – like the 'surrender' option – exacts a huge toll. What will it cost your relationship? Will your husband leave you? Will he make your life a misery? Presumably you wouldn't go so far as dumping him to get what you want – although I do know people who got divorced for less! Dealmakers will only 'conquer' if they hold all the power and believe that they will hold it for a long time to come. Think Robert Mugabe.

## Postpone

A further alternative available to you would be to 'postpone'. You could delay the travel component of your new job for a while, or hold back on having the discussion until your man is in a more receptive frame of mind. Postponing is a favourite tactic of mine. I am quite prepared to wait for the balance of power to shift in my favour, or to postpone in order to give myself more time to think.

Postponement does not work if there is a possibility of the power moving away from you, or when you have a strict deadline to meet. As a catalogue choice, though, it is always worth considering. The wonderful axiom that 'it's easier to ask for forgiveness than permission' is based on the principle of postponement.

## Compromise

You already know what I think of compromise – only doormats are happy to get less than what they want! Of course it is an alternative you can use, but for me it is the most unattractive of choices. If you compromise, or haggle or quibble, as it is alternatively called, it means that not only do you need to settle for less than you want, but the other party will probably not get what *they* want either – there is no value-value deal with this option. Women compromise to avoid conflict, but running away from conflict is not always the right thing to do. More about this later.

A classic story about compromise is King Solomon's solution to the case in which two women were arguing over which one of them was the mother of a baby. Simply cut the baby in half, proposed Solomon. This would obviously have led to the baby's death, had the real mother not offered to stand back and let the other woman have the child. So why, in real life, are we so willing to accept 'half a dead baby'? It is often better to walk away from a deal than to compromise and accept something that does not give you *all* that you want.

In terms of our 'promotion but must travel' case, would it really benefit you to agree to travel only half the time and maybe not achieve your objectives? Or to never be away for more than three days, which would mean no international travel? With compromises of this nature, you would then have a half-happy husband, a disappointed employer and an unhappy you. What is the point? Compromise is the death of good deals.

## Problem-solve

Women like problem-solving, and most of us are quite good at it. We also use problem-solving to help us avoid conflict. In fact, we have become so reliant on problem-solving that we tend to use it, along with a good dose of compromise, as our first means to get the deal. As a result, we close extremely weak deals.

Back to 'promotion but must travel'. With problem-solving, the first step would be to look at where you have common ground with your husband. You want a good job, and he wants you to have one too. A tick in that box. He accepts that your career *and* your family are important to you. Another tick. You are both happy with the big, fat salary you are earning. Tick. You both want what is best for your daughter. Tick again. And so it goes, until you have ticked off all the boxes on which you and your man agree. What remains to be agreed?

You have effectively removed every variable – every area of potential flexibility – from the table, except the most contentious issue: You have to travel. The problem is that the conflict is far more liable to escalate when there is only one major issue on the table than when you can work with, and possibly trade off, several issues. If you are in a situation of high conflict and choose problem-solving as your option, you are likely to intensify the conflict rather than resolve it.

## Conflict-resolve, mediate or arbitrate

This brings us to the subject of conflict resolution. In the real world, conflict-resolution experts are very seldom the same people as negotiation experts. These are two very distinct fields following two very different schools of thought. As I fall into the camp of negotiation rather than conflict resolution, I am unable to offer much in the way of advice here, other than to say that, in our example, where you and your hubby presumably want a decent relationship going forward, it may be advisable to engage the services of a person external to the family unit to resolve the conflict if any of the other options don't work for you.

Whether this is an arbitrator (someone who hears both sides of the story and then makes a decision, like a judge) or a mediator (a person who attempts to find the common ground for the parties and helps them to *compromise*), you would be placing your future in the hands of a third party. The cost this could entail – particularly if the third party is not terribly talented (or is being paid by your husband, perhaps!) – may ultimately be higher than the negotiating option.

We have looked at only a few of the alternatives from the shopping list I gave you, but these are the most common approaches. It is critical that you consider as many alternatives as possible when you're doing a deal. The more time you spend analysing the pros and cons – or costs and benefits – of each and every option, the stronger you will make your position in any deal.

Which of the catalogue options should you try first? *The one that gives you what you want at the least cost*, of course. It's a bit like looking for the perfect pair of Jimmy Choos. If price is your priority, you can try persuading the salesperson to give them to you at the lowest cost, or you might want to postpone buying them until they go on sale. If you really, really need them for a date with Gerard Butler (now we're talking!), you probably don't care what you pay, so you will surrender to the ridiculous price tag. If, on the other hand, you can take 'em or leave 'em, you may just walk away when you see what you have to pay to own them. Conquering, in this case, might be saying to the salesperson: 'I'm having them but I'm not paying' (similar to Lindsay Lohan, who allegedly refused to pay for her champagne in a Los Angeles bar). Me? I'd wait until they were on sale at Selfridges, as the amount I would save on their 75 per cent sale would pay a chunk towards my air ticket to London! The negotiated option would be to say to the store, 'If you give me a discount, I'll buy three pairs.' But that is going to cost you, dahling.

The bottom line is that you are only going to negotiate when it is the cheapest option in terms of getting what you want. It's seldom the first port of call.

## WHAT MAKES NEGOTIATION SO SPECIAL?

So, if negotiation is not the automatic first choice when doing deals, why is such a fuss made about being able to negotiate? It's all to do with the power inherent in the process.

And one of the biggest sources of power in negotiation is that of carrots – or 'incentives', as the authors of *Freakonomics* call them – of giving the person something that they want so that you can get what you want. People are far more flexible when you dangle a juicy carrot or two in front of their noses. A carrot for a carrot. Give to get. It's also a kick-ass way of resolving any conflict with the least possible tension.

> An incentive is a bullet, a lever, a key: an often tiny object with astonishing power to change a situation.
>
> From *Freakonomics* by Steven D. Levitt and Stephen J. Dubner

The more carrots you have, the greater your power. And it's not just their value; it's also the quantity that counts. Think back to the earlier example of the salary package and the benefits you wanted. There was a whole list of variables (marbles or carrot slices) you could use to get the *total* package you desired – you were accepting benefits in exchange for a reduction in the cash part of the salary. The carrot for the employer was, of course, paying you less money but still getting your services. And off you walk with some fabulous benefits – *your* carrots – on which you place a high value.

You are probably realising now that you need to consider which carrots *you* want *and* which you can offer to the other party – it is unlikely that they will be creative enough to come to a meeting with their own bunches of carrots.

Do you think there is anyone, or any entity, that is so powerful that it doesn't have to negotiate? If I ask this question when I am lecturing, the most frequent answer is 'the revenue services'. Okay, we all have to pay tax, but it may surprise you to learn that you can negotiate discounts on any penalties levied against you, payment methods or even the period over which you pay tax. 'Death' is another answer I get to the question. Yes, we are all going to die at some point, but you can cheat physical death to a certain degree with lifestyle, medicine, prayer and affirmations.

Countries, governments, corporations, unions, bosses, employees, customers, suppliers, wives, husbands, parents, children … you name it, they all need to be able to do deals. And the best possible way of going about it is by using negotiation. Even Robert Mugabe negotiates. How do you think he's been able to cling to his despotic presidency for as long as he has?

So, how can you kick-start your negotiating skills? How do you rediscover the brilliant negotiator you were as a child? Here is the first step: The next time someone wants something from you, ask yourself the question: 'What carrot do I want in return for giving this person what they want?' Your sister wants to borrow your pink-leather Versace diva-dress? Lend it to her on condition that she returns it to you dry-cleaned. That sort of thing. Stop giving and start trading – just like a six-year-old child will do instinctively. The more you practise, the easier it becomes. (About the pink Versace: I bought it at a Harrods sale, marked down from £600 to £30 – a 95 per cent reduction. I suspect they made a mistake.)

If you feel a little awkward asking for something in return for a discount, favour or whatever someone wants from you, remind yourself of the expression 'quid pro quo'. If you guess that this is Latin and that it means 'an eye for an eye' or something similar, you would be on the money. The direct translation of 'quid pro quo' is commonly accepted as 'something for something'. This is a concept with which good negotiators are perfectly comfortable. It certainly helped the ancient Romans keep control of their conquered territories for a century or two.

If you are *still* feeling uncomfortable about the process of getting 'something for something', you need to work on three 'soft' issues.

## THREE WAYS TO GET COMFORTABLE WITH TRADING

### 1. Alter your trading mindset

I have never read a book on negotiation or dealmaking that says trading is selfish. I have never heard an expert dealmaker or business guru say that asking for something in return is 'acting in bad faith'. I have yet to discover that looking after your financial well-being is a sin. I have, however, often heard *un*skilled dealmakers make these ridiculous statements.

### 2. Change your relationship with money

There is a common perception that it is bad taste to talk about money. If you have bought into or been brought up with this way of thinking, then you're unlikely to be at ease negotiating – especially when it involves your salary. Abandon this archaic attitude and you will already be better off. Money is not evil – it is the *love* of money that is considered to be the root of all evil! Basically this means that being a greedy bastard is bad. Looking after yourself is good.

### 3. Adjust your negotiating poise

We've spoken about self-assurance and assertiveness in general, but a diva who lacks these two qualities is not likely to feel confident about closing deals. The best way to build confidence is *not* to run away from whatever it is that makes you fearful – it's to grab hold of the monster and tame it. And what better way to go about it than to learn how to become a dealmaker from someone who knows how to sell and negotiate! Ask them to guide and mentor you. But be warned: they may want something in return!

## IS EVERYTHING NEGOTIABLE?

Realistically, do you think that everything is open to negotiation or selling? What about ethics and morals? Or your beliefs and views? Your values and attitudes? If you believe these are *not* up for negotiation, I am going to challenge you on your position. Did you see the movie *Indecent Proposal* with Demi Moore (watch it for the Thierry Mugler dress alone!)? Here is the (tongue-in-cheek) synopsis of the movie from www.amazon.com:

> Yuppie melodrama that poses the conundrum of whether the loving husband of an equally loving wife will accept $1 million to allow his wife to spend one night with a billionaire who looks like Robert Redford. Demi Moore and Woody Harrelson play Diana and David Murphy, high-school sweethearts who marry and who are doing very well – Diana is a successful real-estate agent, and David is an idealistic architect who has built a dream house by the ocean – until the recession hits. Suddenly, David loses his job, and they can't make the mortgage payments. Dead broke, they borrow $5 000 from David's father and head to Las Vegas to try to win money to pay the mortgage on their house. At first, they get $25 000 ahead – but inevitably the house always wins, and they end up losing it all. While Diana is in the fancy casino boutique trying to lift some candy, she is spotted by billionaire John Gage (Robert Redford), who is immediately attracted to her. John invites Diana and David to an opulent party, and it is there that John offers David $1 million for a night with his wife.

Be honest now: If you were being offered $1 million for your partner, would you take it? If you can't get your mind around Robert Redford with your man, pretend that it is Demi Moore who's making the offer.

**If your answer is NO, read on** ... *But you are about to lose your house!* Still no? But why not? Are you jealous then? Still a 'no'? It is because of your principles? In that case, you have a very dirty mind, *madame*! Nowhere in the movie or in the synopsis above does anyone mention S.E.X. Can it be that you don't trust your partner to keep his grabby little hands to himself? You think I am missing the point, don't you?

Let me ask you this question – and don't dare answer 'none': Under what conditions would you let your partner spend the night with Robert Redford (or Demi Moore)? What if there was no physical contact? What if you chaperoned them (or watched – who knows what floats your boat!)? No way? Okay, you are clearly on a moral crusade. Now imagine Robert Redford (or Demi) holding your man by the ankles as he dangles over the edge at the top of Sandton City and saying, 'If you don't let him spend the night with me, I'll drop him.' Ah, but that's a completely different situation, you say. Not so. We're haggling about the price – his life or $1 million. The issue – spending the night – remains the same.

Believe it or not, I am not just being flippant. *Everything is negotiable*, but it does very much depend on the *cost*. If the price is not right, you won't do the deal. But sometimes you may not *have* a choice (think figurative life or death).

If you're not prepared to accept the offer simply because $1 million dollars is not enough, see below.

**If your answer is YES, read on** ... You are a girl after my own heart. What, though, if you could have got more than a million bucks? After all, that was just the first offer. Would Robert (or Demi) have been prepared to go up to two, five or ten million? Or give you the yacht instead? Maybe you could have introduced a sliding scale of action, with different price tags for different favours? Being such a saint, I would unselfishly have offered to take my man's place with Robert Redford for the night, wrinkly or not.

Now test your friends.

There is, of course, a very serious point to this fun example. A skilled dealmaker recognises that everything is open to negotiation or persuasion (or any other option from the catalogue), but they decide whether the deal is worth doing or not. Sometimes the personal price may be too high and you will want to say no – but the truth is, an expert dealmaker *never* says no. They just keep asking for something in return. The more outrageous the demand, the more outrageous their price.

And now a story to warm your heart – and to make you smile the next time you open a bottle of wine.

> Sally was driving home from one of her business trips in Northern Arizona when she saw an elderly Navajo woman walking on the side of the road. As the trip was a long and quiet one, she stopped the car and asked the Navajo woman if she would like a ride. With a silent nod of thanks, the woman got into the car.
> 
> Resuming the journey, Sally tried in vain to make a bit of small talk with the woman. The old woman just sat silently, looking intently at everything she saw, studying every little detail, until she noticed a brown bag on the seat next to Sally.
> 
> 'What in bag?' asked the old woman. Sally looked down at the brown bag and said, 'It's a bottle of wine. I got it for my husband.'
> 
> The Navajo woman was silent for another moment or two. Then, speaking with the quiet wisdom of an elder, she said:
> 
> 'Good trade.'

From http://riotwineblog.com

## DO YOU GET WHAT YOU DESERVE, OR DESERVE WHAT YOU GET?

There are *four lies women tell themselves* that hinder them from getting what they want in dealmaking and in life:

1. I don't deserve it – I'm not worthy.
2. I can't sell.
3. I'm a rubbish negotiator.
4. I'm no good with conflict.

We have touched on all these topics already, but here are the lessons that every self-respecting deal diva needs to learn.

## 1. I'm not worthy

And here she is again – the friggin' doormat. We have bashed this beast on the head with our handbags; we have stomped on her in our stilettos, threatened her life and chased her off with a Choo. If you tick one, yes even *one*, of these boxes, go back to Chapter 1 and start again. Do not pass go. Do not collect your 'diva' certificate. Do not do anything until you have stopped with the 'I'm not worthy' routine. The only person who ever looked cute doing this was Mike Myers in *Wayne's World*.

| I AM NOT WORTHY, I AM NOT WORTHY | ACCEPT |
|---|---|
| 1. I am not concerned about earning the same as a man for doing the same job. I am just lucky to have a job. | |
| 2. Men are the breadwinners, so they should earn more than their female counterparts. | |
| 3. My man is financially astute and far better qualified to look after my finances than me. | |
| 4. I just can't get my pretty little head around numbers. | |
| 5. I already have so much that I don't need something in return when someone wants concessions from me. | |
| 6. Nobody will like me if I take a firm position. | |
| 7. I will compromise my gentleness if I am assertive. | |
| 8. I don't want to be seen as greedy. | |
| 9. If I work hard, I won't need to ask – I will automatically be noticed and rewarded. | |
| 10. Talking about money is very crass and makes me feel like a prostitute. | |

## 2. I can't sell

As I say in *Work Diva*, you can't just sit around and hope that someone will notice you and choose you for his bride, recruit you for the job of a lifetime or psychically sense your potential. You have to *sell* yourself. You have to be able to convince someone else – whether through your verbal, physical, sexual or intellectual skills – that you are who they want. We have established that *everyone* can sell. Without this ability, you would have no jobs, dates, friends, lovers or network. You would not be able to function properly in life.

Ironically, most women are more comfortable selling than negotiating, despite their protestations about never having worked in sales. When I was a human resources executive (I know, I know – it's sort of like letting the dog look after the cats), I was offered the agency for a world-class sales process programme. I was dead keen but extremely concerned about not being able to sell. The senior executive to whom I reported promised to teach me to sell. Guess what? He pointed out to me how I had been selling my whole life long! Once I got over my mental block, not only did I become one of the top five salespeople in the company, I *loved* selling! It was exciting, stimulating, profitable *and* hair-raising.

If you want to improve your selling skills, go on a course or two, read a few books, hang out with salespeople (found in fun places) – kiss the blooming Blarney Stone if you must. But it is only when you understand the power inherent in selling that the world will be laid at your beautifully shod feet.

## 3. I can't negotiate

Nonsense. Ask your parents (if you are lucky enough to still have them around) whether you were any good at getting what you wanted when you were a kid.

They will tell you that you started exhibiting selling skills at the age of two (screaming your head off in the trolley at the supermarket to encourage them to sign the order – i.e. buy you a chocolate).

At age three you could already persuade (or plead, as in, '*Please* can I have a chocolate?').

By the age of four you were a master manipulator (more selling skills – 'I love you, Mom, please can I have a chocolate? If I was the Mom I would buy a chocolate for *you*!').

At five you were already a negotiator ('If you buy the chocolate for me, I will share it with you.').

Aged six years old, you were an expert negotiator ('If you take me to the park on Saturday, I will go to bed early/eat my peas/not pull my sister's hair/be good/not embarrass you in front of your friends/stop kissing the dog/not throw stones …').

By eight you were a persistent, creative and flexible little beggar who could sell and negotiate, all in one transaction.

Now tell me that you don't know how to negotiate! And being able to negotiate is *brilliant*! A skilled dealmaker knows how far to push for a salary increase. She is able to get the maximum possible price when she wants to sell her house or car, for example. She can get customers to buy from her without giving away discounts. She can negotiate price reductions like a *real diva*.

## 4. I'm no good with conflict

Women are nurturers by nature. All of us. I have never had a broody moment in my life, but put a small animal in front of me and I am cuddling it in a nanosecond. If women have been designed to promote and sustain life, it should be no surprise that they shy away from conflict and fighting.

Scientific evidence supports this. In his book *Mind Wide Open*, Steven Johnson states: 'They [men and women] have reliably different amounts of gray matter; some areas linked to sexuality and aggressions are larger in men than in women.' An article by Sven Lunsche in the *Wits Business School Journal*, Vol. 3, 2009, titled *If Women Were In Charge*, suggests that it's the higher levels of testosterone in men that make them more aggressive in business. These are just two examples from thousands of studies.

That women are pre-programmed to nurture does not exonerate them from having to deal with conflict. If women want to abdicate this responsibility to men, they cannot be crybabies when they are not taken seriously or are treated iniquitously. They need to find an approach that is not counter-instinctual but that can constructively deal with conflict. If they simply do what they have always done – make the usual sacrifices and concessions to ease the friction – they will continue to get lousy deals, and will win no respect in the process. Problem-solving does not help either: When common ground is 'ticked' away, it leaves only the flammable, contentious issues on the table.

What is the answer? Combining assertiveness with processes like selling and negotiation gives women the tools they need to take control of conflict situations. When a woman is in control, she is also able to manage her emotions more appropriately. Richard 'Tricky Dick' Nixon (*American president; 1913–1994*) was recorded on White House audiotapes explaining why he would not appoint a woman to the US Supreme Court: 'I don't think a woman should be in any government job whatsoever … mainly because they are erratic. And emotional. Men are erratic and emotional, too, but the point is a woman is more likely to be.' What a Dick.

Feeling in control and minimising emotion give a woman far more confidence in conflict situations.

Conflict is destructive when it is left to fester and breed and escalate out of control. The human form of conflict is personified by the character Alex (played by Glenn Close) in *Fatal Attraction*. 'I will not be ignored,' she says, and proceeds to boil the bunny. Perhaps an extreme example, but don't avoid conflict – take control and end its misery.

## DISCOMBOBULATED, DEAREST?

If you are feeling somewhat overwhelmed by all the information you have been given and disconcerted by the adjustments you need to make, never mind panicky about what you still need to learn to become a deal diva, *relax!* This anxiety is perfectly normal. It's a psychological state called 'conscious competence', which is basically your brain upgrading one of its programmes. Here is how www.wikipedia.com explains it:

> In psychology, the four stages of competence, or the 'conscious competence' learning model, relates to the psychological states involved in the process of progressing from incompetence to competence in a skill.

Stage 1: Unconscious Incompetence
The individual neither understands nor knows how to do something, nor recognises the deficit, nor has a desire to address it.

Stage 2: Conscious Incompetence
Though the individual does not understand or know how to do something, he or she does recognise the deficit, without yet addressing it.

Stage 3: Conscious Competence
The individual understands or knows how to do something. However, demonstrating the skill or knowledge requires a great deal of consciousness or concentration.

Stage 4: Unconscious Competence
The individual has had so much practice with a skill that it becomes 'second nature' and can be performed easily (often without concentrating too deeply). He or she may or may not be able teach it to others, depending upon how and when it was learned.

Take heart, dear diva. On the strength of what you have learnt so far, you are already somewhere between the end of stage 2 and the beginning of stage 3 (assuming you are learning a lot of this for the first time). Just don't give up! The furthest this *Deal Diva* journey can take you is to the end of stage 3, so not far now. It's nearly time for that pina colada.

# Chapter 4

## WOMEN AND THE FINE ART OF COMMUNICATION

> 'Hello wall.'
> – *Shirley Valentine (from the play by Willy Russell; 1986)*

You should be very pleased with yourself. You've been exposed to some fairly hairy content – the sort of lessons you would receive if you were doing Women's Studies at a business school. Take a look at how far you have progressed in gathering the tools and knowledge you need to be a real deal diva. You now know:
- How to be a goddess instead of a doormat.
- How to value yourself and the work that you do.
- That persuasion, and especially negotiation, is the skill that expert dealmakers rely on most of the time.
- That you have a catalogue of choices you can use to close deals.
- That everything is open to negotiation, depending on the price!
- How to make the perfect pina colada. (Okay, maybe you wouldn't learn that at business school!)

Now take your feet out of your killer heels for a moment and put on your comfy slippers. We are going back to familiar territory, so relax while you can.

It's time to take another yummy bite of the 'dealmaker' definition – the communication chunk. Earlier I made the statement that women are excellent communicators and that the plan is to take you from first class to fantastic. Just in case you've forgotten the definition, here it is again:

> A person skilled in using instinct, processes and expertise in primarily negotiation, selling and communication, and able to leverage or adjust the balance of power to bring closure to transactions that usually benefit all parties.
>
> © The Dealmaker Programmes Company

Anecdotal evidence suggests that women are more effective communicators than men. One just has to think about the 'conversations' Shirley Valentine manages to have with the *wall*. It is how women use this gift in the context of being a deal diva that can take them to dizzying new heights.

According to the experts, 'communication' is the imparting or exchanging of information, either verbally or non-verbally. *Verbal* communication is concerned with words, and includes speech, sign language and writing; *non-verbal* communication, on the other hand, encompasses wordless messages such as gestures, body language, posture, facial expressions and eye contact.

*Verbal* communication works on two levels: what we say *consciously* and what we say *unconsciously*. With conscious verbal communication you are cognisant of the words you are choosing and using. *Unconscious* verbal communication is when we include words without being aware that we have actually said them. They are usually simple, descriptive words. For example, 'I really, really want the deal.' Sounds normal, doesn't it? Using the word 'really' twice, though, signals desperation, whereas using the word only once demonstrates eagerness. How about: 'I want around about R90 000 for my car'? Does the seller want R90 000, or more, or less? The words 'around about' are innocent enough, but what is the seller actually communicating? More on this later.

In *Work Diva* I discussed the verbal and non-verbal aspects of communication, but only touched on a third dimension – that of instinctual, intuitive or telepathic communication. While the pundits may argue that telepathic communication falls into the 'non-verbal' category, I'm not convinced. From what I have seen, read and been told, people pick up information that could not possibly be gleaned from body language alone. Besides, telepathic communication also takes place when people are *not* in each other's company, or listening to one another – or even when there is no link in the space–time continuum.

The most reliable form of communication is unquestionably verbal communication, so that is where we will begin. If you are in any doubt as to the importance of words, here is a delightful story about a phrasebook from *The Heroic Book of Failures* by Stephen Pile.

The Worst Phrasebook

Pedro Carolino is one of the greats. In 1883 he wrote an English-Portuguese phrasebook despite having little or no command of the English Language.

His greatly recommended book *The New Guide of the Conversation in Portuguese and English* has been reprinted under the title *English as She Is Spoke*.

After a brief dedication:

'We expect then, who the little book (for the care what we wrote him, and for her typographical correction) that may be worth the acceptation of the studious persons, and especially of the youth, at which we dedicate him particularly.'

Carolino kicks off with some 'Familiar phrases', which the Portuguese holidaymaker might find useful. Among these are:

Dress your hairs

Exculpate me by your brother's

She make the prude

He has tost his all good

He then moves on to 'Familiar Dialogues', which include 'For to wish the good morning', and 'For to visit a sick'. In the section on 'Anecdotes', Carolino offers the following, guaranteed to enthral any listener:

'One eyed was laied against a man which had good eyes that he saw better than him. The party was accepted. I had gain, over said to the one eyed: why I se you two eyes, and you not look me who one.'

It is difficult to top that, but Carolino manages in a useful section of 'Idiotisms and proverbs'. These include:

He eat to coaches
The stone as roll not heap up not foam
The dog than bark not bite

Carolino's particular genius was aided by the fact that he did not possess an English-Portuguese dictionary. However, he did possess Portuguese-French and French-English dictionaries through which he dragged his original expressions. The results yield language of originality and great beauty. Is there anything in conventional English which could equal the vividness of 'To craunch a marmoset'?

## CONSCIOUS VERBAL COMMUNICATION – WHAT WOMEN SAY

I am going to be pretty pedantic about the conscious use of words in dealmaking. Negotiators, in particular, choose their words very carefully. Consider hostage negotiations for a moment – one wrong word and people could lose their lives. In any important transaction, the use of precise wording is just as important. A wrong word here could mean the death of your deal. Success *does* lie in semantics.

Think before you speak (and before you write) *and* pay careful attention to what the other person is saying. (More about the other person when we talk about unconscious verbal communication.) Thinking about what you want to say does mean that you need to *consciously plan* what you're going to say – right down to the exact words you intend to use. The upside of this is that when you think carefully about your words, you are less likely to say something you'll regret.

In presenting The Dealdiva™ programme for women, my organisation spends a disproportionate amount of time focusing on which words to use when doing deals. Carefully chosen words help to increase the control you have when you sell or negotiate. They also enable timid women to be more assertive, and aggressive women to tone down the testicle crushing. If choosing your words slows you down, fabulous!

Slow is best when you are doing deals, especially when there is tension or conflict. Can you remember the last couple of arguments you had – with your parents, partner, children, staff or boss, for instance? As the argument got more heated, the tempo would have increased, allowing more and more unconscious words to slip in. Faster = less time to think = 'bugger, I wish I hadn't said that'. Watch those words!

What you say and what the other party hears might not be the same thing, so in addition to diligently choosing your words, you must check that the other person understands exactly what you mean. To do this you need to ask questions, to summarise and to confirm – point by point – to ensure that crazy assumptions or misinterpretations have not crept into the discussion *à la* Sēnor Pedro Carolino.

When you are negotiating, there are a few words you should use – and then there are those you should try to avoid. We will cover these in detail when we explore the face-to-face aspect of negotiation but, in the meanwhile, would you like to hazard a guess as to which is the most powerful word a negotiator can use? It's the little word '*if*', believe it or not.

- *If* you take me out to a restaurant tonight, then I will make dinner for the rest of the week.
- *If* you want to go to the rave on Saturday, then you must wash my car by Friday.
- *If* you go and bath, you can watch television for half an hour afterwards.
- *If* you give me a 20 per cent increase, then I will accept the additional responsibilities.
- *If* you want that discount, then I want this volume.
- *If*… then …

Negotiation is about trading. Trading is giving to get. Giving to get is '*if* you do this for me, *then* I will do that for you'. Quid pro quo.

A hilarious and lovely Brit with whom I taught Scotwork Negotiation Skills in the UK and USA for a couple of years tells the story of a negotiation he had with his nine-year-old son. 'If you don't make me eat my cabbage,' the boy said, 'then I won't embarrass you in front of your friends the next time they come round.' This colleague is also the person who taught me how to encourage kids to eat their cabbage (i.e. to get someone to do what you want them to do): promise them chocolate for dessert. But, he warned, never give them the choccies first. Duh – this seems so obvious! How come, then, when we are negotiating, we are quite happy to offer the chocolate first?

When you say, 'If you do this for me, then I will do that for you,' you communicate clearly to the other person that you will give them something they want (e.g. chocolate) if they give you what *you* want (i.e. eat the cabbage). I think that this is a far more honest (and reliable) way of dealing with someone than giving them chocolate in the hope that they will do what you want. It is much less manipulative. Sure, we like to give the good news first. We prefer to say, 'I'll be happy to accept the additional responsibility, boss.' The problem is that the boss rushes off to her next meeting before you've had the chance to add, 'But then I want an increase.' You must tell the other person what you want before you agree to give her chocolate. *Think before you speak.*

For interest's sake, any idea which is the most overused word? It's the word 'I'. While self-promotion and self-confidence are important, be careful of being an 'I-specialist', as I call such people: 'I did this' or 'I think that'. People stop caring after the fifteenth 'I'. When I am teaching new lecturers to present The Dealmaker™ programmes, they are taught to balance establishing their credibility with being an I-specialist. The best way in which to do this is to share their 'I screwed up' stories with the delegates, along with examples of how things should be done. Nobody likes a braggart.

## UNCONSCIOUS VERBAL COMMUNICATION – WHAT WOMEN MEAN

When we talk, we unwittingly drop little 'clues', or 'verbal cues', or 'signals' into a conversation. No matter how well we prepare our conscious words, we are unlikely to be able to eradicate all of the unconscious communication. Obviously, with written communication you have a far greater chance of reducing unconscious signals, as you have time to review what you want to say. Not so with direct conversations. A few savvy operators can control their words to this extent, but the trick is not to stop yourself giving the clues – it's to pick up the clues that you are given. Not sure what I'm talking about? Let's expand on the example I used earlier. When you see an advert in the newspaper that reads: 'BMW for sale – R90 000 o.n.c.o.', what is the clue? It's the 'o.n.c.o.' – 'or nearest cash offer' – which means that the R90 000 is negotiable.

Imagine you are talking to someone on the phone and you ask him what he wants for an item he is selling (I don't mean the fixed pricing in shops). He will probably say, 'I want in the region of R5 000,' or, 'I need to clear about R5 000.' Both of these statements hold clues, albeit subtle ones. *'In the region of'* means 'negotiable'. *'About* R5 000' means negotiable. Why, then, do we write down 'R5 000' on our notepads and not ± R5 000? Because we have missed the clues!

Clues don't have to be words. They can be intonations, pauses or stammering. Change your tone when you read the following three statements by emphasising the italicised words:

1. I can't do *that* for you.
2. I can't do that for *you*.
3. *I* can't do that for you.

Where are the clues in these statements?
   Answers:
1. But I might be able to do something else.
2. Perhaps I shall do it for someone else.
3. Maybe my boss can do that for you.

Clues can range from the blatantly obvious to the obscure. The trick, as I said, is to spot them rather than to stop yourself from giving them. To recognise clues, you need to listen very carefully to what the other person is saying – you need to be 'in the moment', as New Agers advise. It is an art, but the more you practise, the better – and the richer – you will get.

What should you do when you spot a clue? You need to explore it. 'I'm not going to buy you a drink,' says the cute guy with whom you are chatting in the bar. Rather than storming off in a huff or throwing a hissy fit, ask, 'Why not?' You might find out that he:

- Intends buying you more than one drink.
- Would love to buy you a drink but has left his wallet at home.
- Wants *you* to buy him a drink.
- Is just not that into you.
- Would prefer to take you to dinner.
- Does not approve of women who drink.
- Thinks you will order something too expensive.

If it's because he thinks you'll order something pricey, dump him immediately – no diva wants to date a man who is stingy, or who suspects she is a hooker working for the bar! If he's just being a rude git, stab your stiletto heel into his toes. If he won't tell you why he won't buy you a drink, he's either married or the seriously uncommunicative type – neither of whom you want anyway.

So, before you dive straight in and punish Cute Guy, it is best to find out *why* he doesn't want to buy you the drink. If you read the signals incorrectly, you may miss out on a hot date, or maybe it *is* stiletto time after all.

Avoid the temptation to point out a clue that you have spotted to the person who has given it to you. He may get embarrassed about his being so transparent and dig in on a position – and intransigence will ruin everything. Simply explore the clue, expand on it and then make a counter-offer.

Why do I say you shouldn't worry too much about trying *not* to give clues? Clues are signs of flexibility, and flexibility in negotiation is good. If you look back to the list of six ways in which children outmanoeuvre adults, there it is. Besides, to try to control both the unconscious *and* the conscious words you use in deal-making is a very tall order.

## BODY LANGUAGE – WHAT WOMEN SUGGEST

You are sitting at the bar (again) and another guy comes over to chat to you. You flick your hair and lick your lips. Are you doing this consciously or unconsciously? It could be either. What if the poor chap hits on you, thinking that you were giving him the come-on, but you were just getting your hair out of your eyes and licking off a blob of salt from your margarita? Sore toes for him for sure.

I am no body language specialist (there are lots of good books and articles available on the subject), but I do know that to interpret body language successfully you need to know what the person's normal behaviour is, observe any change in this behaviour and decode said change.

Body language is strongly tied to culture, though differences between the genders, and even age groups, should not be discounted. One perfectly acceptable sign in one country may be a significant insult in another. I learnt this the hard way. Two very good books you can read on the subject are *Kiss, Bow or Shake Hands* by Terri Morrison and Wayne A. Conway, and *When Cultures Collide* by Richard D. Lewis.

Another body language example: You see a man waiting at a bus stop. You do not know him. He is standing with his arms folded across his chest. What does this mean? That he is hostile or closed off? What if I now mention that the weather is chilly? Could he be trying to keep himself warm? And now I tell you about the gorgeous woman he is watching. Is he trying to make his pecs look bigger? Maybe he is just resting his arms on his large stomach. Who knows? You would have to ask him why he is standing the way he is – and is that when he shows you the horrible sore on his wrist?

Verbal communication is a more reliable communication mechanism than body language, because words – although also at the mercy of societal mores – can be controlled to a large extent. Non-verbal communication, on the other hand, is subject to interpretation – and I would prefer not to rely on reading between the lips. This is not to say you should completely discount body language – just do your homework before you try to use it as a predictor of how another person is feeling.

## ESOTERIC COMMUNICATION, GUT INSTINCT, FEMININE INTUITION

Have you ever had a distinct 'feeling' about a deal – whether it was a business transaction or a personal matter (such as buying a house or a car, or taking a job) – that either cautioned or encouraged you? Did you follow your intuition, or did you ignore it? What were the consequences of either decision?

In communication, there is a dimension beyond the verbal and non-verbal that needs to be considered too – that of 'alternative' or esoteric communication. You can call it gut instinct, feminine intuition, sixth sense, psychic transmission or telepathy. 'Telepathy' is also a good choice, as it describes the communication between minds by some means other than sensory perception. The other word I like is 'intuition', and not just because of the association with *feminine* intuition.

Why 'intuition'? When I was working with my company's business partners, Innovate+Grow Group, in Vienna in 2009, I had an interesting debate with Peter Sicher, the dashing managing partner of the company. Peter is a brilliant academic and intellectual. I am always going to come second in any debate with him. Anyhow, Peter was disputing my interchangeable use of the words 'instinct' and 'intuition' to describe alternative abilities in dealmaking. Peter insisted that 'intuition' was the right word. There I was, thinking, 'His first language is German. How would he know?' But blow me down, he was right. As usual. 'Instinct' is defined as 'an inborn pattern of behaviour or innate capability', whereas 'intuition' is 'knowing or sensing without the use of rational processes' (source: www.thefreedictionary.com).

On to telepathy. A couple of years ago I attended an animal communication course led by the phenomenal Anna Breytenbach. Anna, who is as beautiful on the inside as she is on the outside, is the person you will see on television or hear on the radio talking about, for instance, why the pilot whales beached themselves at Kommetjie in Cape Town, in May 2009. (If you're interested, it was because the whales had been contaminated by toxins in the sea – they were dying a slow and excruciating death – and they wanted to end their suffering together. And there we were, the genuinely concerned humans, trying to put them back into the sea.) Anyhow, Anna taught us to calm our minds and then took us through a process where we connected telepathically with the soul of the animal with which we wanted to communicate, including pets that had passed from this realm back into spirit.

If you're a sceptic like me, try it before you dismiss it. What I saw and heard defies explanation. The point is, if we are able to communicate with animals telepathically (and there is evidence to suggest we can), why can't we communicate with our fellow humans in this way? Some people can and do, but the majority of us have lost this ability. Sigmund Freud (*Austrian neurologist and founder of psychoanalysis; 1856–1939*) called telepathy a 'regressive and primitive faculty that has mostly been lost in evolution'. (If I stated the reasons why I believe people have lost their psychic ability, I fear I'd be burnt at the stake.)

Scientists tend to conduct research into telepathic communication with isolated societies, and one such study was done with a remote Aboriginal community in Australia. The scientists, after establishing that this group of Aboriginal people had never tasted certain tropical fruits, gave one person a banana to eat. The banana-eater had to communicate telepathically the *taste* of the banana to his tribesmen. His compatriots were then given a selection of fruit that none of them had tasted before, and on the strength of the telepathic message, were asked to identify the banana. They scored 100 per cent.

The bottom line is this: Pay attention to what you sense. Don't ignore it. Just because you can't explain what you are picking up does not mean that it is flaky. More and more research is being done into the importance of alternative forms of communication in our lives, including in the business environment (and if this New Age 'touchy-feely stuff' doesn't frighten the bigoted old dinosaurs out of business, nothing will!).

So, whether you want to ascribe the information you gather – which is neither verbal nor non-verbal – to a primal ability like gut instinct, or to 'knowing' through feminine intuition, or to an alternative sensory perception such as telepathy, listen carefully to what your instinct has to say!

If you're keen to know more about esoteric communication, there are plenty of internet articles you can read, such as 'Trust Gut Instincts and Intuition' on http://www.scribd.com/doc/14885405/Trust-Gut-Instincts-and-Intuition.

## THE DEBATING SOCIETY

It's all well and good knowing the differences between verbal, non-verbal and alternative communication, but where does this fit into the wonderful world of selling and negotiating? Much more time in dealmaking is spent in debate (or discussion, if you prefer) than in the actual process of trading, so we need to have a tight grip on the communication aspects of the process.

The Pareto Principle (you know, the 80/20 rule) applies in dealmaking too. Eighty per cent of the time available is spent in discussion and persuasion, leaving 20 per cent to negotiate or close the deal. This might *seem* fine, as we know how important communication is – and we know that spending time persuading someone is usually a lot less expensive than negotiating with them – but the discussion part of the deal is not always constructive. And if it's not constructive, valuable time is wasted going round and round in circles when we should actually be focusing on getting the deal.

Why is so *much* time spent debating when we should be negotiating? Firstly, many women prefer the chit-chat to the decisiveness of closing a deal. Secondly, for a few of us, the fighting is part of the fun – trying to outwit the other guy gives us a buzz. Lastly, people who lack confidence in their negotiating skills are happier to stay on the safe ground of conversation and persuasion rather than get into trading. The problem is that pointless debate can lead to inconclusive or less-than-optimal deals. *Constructive* discussion, on the other hand, is an essential component of good dealmaking.

Don't be fooled into thinking that a dealmaker meets with the other party, the two have a discussion and then they conclude the deal. A deal can take years to bring to closure. An acquisition I was driving in Germany took two years to finalise. A similar deal in the UK took seven months. First there is all the planning, then there is a series of meetings with everyone from the other side to both parties' lawyers, accountants, financiers and advisors, and then back to the other party, then more planning, and then it starts all over again. One can get quite dizzy before the negotiation even begins! Only when you are finished with all the discussion and debate – you can see where the 80 per cent comes in – will you have anything that resembles your eventual deal.

To make the absolute most of the debate time, you must control the interaction. You need to use the time to try to persuade the other party to give you what you want, but if this is not working, you need to switch to negotiation. While you are persuading, though, you should also be obtaining information for a negotiation, just in case the persuasion option fails. You then use the information you have gathered to negotiate the closing of the deal.

In order to keep the discussion constructive, here are the most important outcomes you should be targeting in order to control the communication process in dealmaking.

## SEVEN ESSENTIAL OBJECTIVES FOR DEBATE
### 1. Persuade and position value propositions
You know that persuasion should usually be your first choice to help you get what you want at the lowest cost, so debate time should ideally be used to convince the other party to agree to what you ask of them. It might be that they purchase $x$ from you, or give you $y$ discount, or agree to preferential terms on something you want to buy. To increase their success using persuasion, expert salespeople develop arguments around what they call 'value propositions'. Bear in mind that this is not just relevant to 'selling' per se. If you are buying a house and you want to convince the seller to include, say, the furniture in the sale, you effectively become a salesperson.

A value proposition describes your or your company's unique selling point, or differentiator. It's the compelling reason why someone would give you what you want. A value proposition is *always* written from the other party's perspective.

For example, if you are interviewing for a job you desperately want, you are not going to say to the interviewer, 'I really, really want this job.' You need to look at the world through *their* eyes and say something like, 'My knowledge of your industry means that you won't need to train me, which will save you a huge amount of money and time.' There's a big difference between the two, not so? Make sure you work on a few value propositions, because different issues are important to different people. The financial person may be delighted with the savings your ready knowledge will bring, but the human resources executive may need reassurance that you are not a job-hopper. In this case your value proposition would be: 'My stable track record will mean that you won't need to be recruiting this position again for a long time to come.'

How do you know what the other person will value? Do. Your. Homework.

## 2. Present (and receive) arguments to substantiate your case

Presenting a virtuoso value proposition may not be enough to convince the other person to give you what you want. You need to be able to back this up with a whole raft of other incentives and information. Why bother with a value proposition then, you might ask. The value proposition is your foot in the door. It's what will get you onto the shortlist. It's the compelling reason for the other person to buy into your deal. This does mean planning, preparing and doing your homework!

Remember Cute Guy from the bar? By asking him *why* he would not buy you a drink, you got valuable information that helped you decide what your next step should be. The same applies here. Ask lots of questions of the other party to make sure that the information you present back to them is meaningful and addresses their issues. Guess what? You also need to prepare these questions in advance. Obviously you can't prepare them all – you will need to ask questions on the spot that you couldn't have anticipated – but be sure that you know what you need to know. And when they tell you what their issues are, or give you answers to your questions, *listen*! The information you get may result in your going away and rethinking your whole plan. If that's what you need to do, do it.

## 3. Test understanding and assumptions – on both sides

The time you spend in discussion, or debate, with the other person is the ideal opportunity to make sure that she appreciates what you want. Equally essential is to check your understanding of what *she* wants. What you say and what the other party hears might not be the same thing, and vice versa. The best way to check that no confusion has crept in is to ask clarifying questions throughout the discussion – both impromptu and prepared questions.

Have you ever heard the expression 'to *assume* makes an *ass* out of *u* and *me*'?

That's ass poo, quite frankly. It is very important, in any conversation you have, to make assumptions. However, you *must* – read my lips: you *must* – check your assumptions. If a customer says that he has a R1-million budget to spend on office plants, don't just assume that the budget is for this year – *check* that it is for this year. Making the assumption regarding the budget is good practice; not checking your assumption may end up with you looking like the proverbial horse's bottom.

And for good measure, check for assumptions that *they* might be making as well. Any misunderstandings that you can clear up while you are still in debate mode will serve you well as the deal progresses.

### 4. Recap and summarise points and markers

In the same vein, it's vital to confirm what has been discussed and agreed on throughout the deal – right to the very end. Summaries are like milestones or road signs. Imagine you are driving from Johannesburg to Cape Town. There are sections on the trip where there are no petrol stations for hundreds of kilometres. If you don't know how far you've got to go to the next stop, you may well run out of fuel. Not something you want to do, say, in the middle of the Karoo late at night. Dealmaking is the same. If you don't use summaries to check where you are, you might find your deal spluttering because nobody took stock of how far you have come or how far you've still got to go. Don't rely on the other guy to recap – if you keep the markers, *you* keep control of the discussion.

One VIP (very important point): *Summaries must be objective.* If you summarise in your favour, it is just a form of persuasion, and the other person may feel the need to counter-persuade. Summaries are meant to help move your discussions forward – to stop everyone from going around in circles, in other words. It is only when the other party trusts your summaries – and they need to be objective to be trustworthy – that summaries are worth their salt.

So, in summary, summaries help to:
- Give structure to the discussions.
- Check the clarity and understanding of everyone – no Pedros in the room.

- Get everyone focused on whatever the key issues might be.
- Keep stock of what has been discussed and what still needs to be discussed.
- Identify the markers – the milestones – in your discussions.
- Confirm areas of agreement and what still needs to be agreed.

## 5. Get and give information

Information is power, or so the saying goes. It's not actually information that is power; the power lies in how you *use* the information – or *don't* use it. It's also about having the *right* information. The key to using debate time effectively when you are doing deals is to get – and give – information.

Let's 'get' information first. You need to know what you need to know, so give thought beforehand to the information you need to gather. Information for information's sake is pointless. What is the best way to extract information? It's to *ask*! And that means preparing the questions in advance. If you don't know who to ask for information, there are unlimited sources you can use – the internet, websites, annual reports, going to the relevant office and reading the magazines lying around in reception, chatting to the receptionist ... Be creative!

Now let's talk about 'giving' information. If using information properly gives you power, it makes sense that you would want to provide the other person with data that substantiates or helps your case. Again, this means planning. You will find, dear diva, that more than half the roads in dealmaking lead back to planning. However, you must also know what information you do *not* want to disclose. This would be information that could weaken your case. You need a strategy on how you will keep this information private, including how you will handle questions on the information that you do not want to divulge. Do you know how to divert attention away from sensitive subjects? It's covered in the section on power a bit later on.

## 6. Set expectations

Following close on the heels of getting and giving information is a little tactic called *setting expectations*, which I learnt when I was working for Scotwork Negotiating

Skills. When you structure or set expectations, you get the other person thinking in the way you want her to think. This is best done early on in the discussions. Setting expectations can range from making strong and specific proposals to subtle hints and suggestions. Choose whatever style will work best for you to direct the other party's thinking.

A very simple example: If you have little in the way of savings but are earning a monthly salary, you should tell the car dealer upfront that you will be able to afford the monthly repayments but will find it extremely difficult to pay a deposit on the car. From the outset, the dealer will have heard your issues and should, if he is a professional, factor these into financing options that do not require a large deposit.

Don't tell lies. If you fib and the other person finds out, you will damage your credibility and your case. The other party will mistrust everything else you've said, whether you told them the truth or not. If you are just at the dealer for a joyride in a new car, don't lie about this. Tell the salesperson you want to test-drive a car because you plan to buy one at some point. And don't pitch up in your schlumpy clothes wanting to drive the latest Aston Martin. Richard Branson may be able to get away with looking like something the cat threw up, but can you?

## 7. Test your negotiation strategy and plan

The benefit of having conversations and debates in dealmaking is to obtain information that will help you close the deal more effectively. You should have done some preparation before going into a meeting, but it may well happen that, in the process of the discussions, you find that your preconceived plans and ideas are meaningless.

If you do obtain information that substantially changes your position or strategy, throw out all the hard work and planning you have done and start again. It is infinitely better to postpone or adjourn the meeting and go away to rethink everything than to carry on with a negotiation that you know will fail. If you completely ignore what the other party has said and you stick to your original but irrelevant plan, you may not get a second chance when everything goes pop. And go pop it will.

When you have a well-thought-out plan, you know exactly what you want – including how high you can push and how low you can go. You know where you can be flexible and you know what you expect in return for the flexibility – and you have a list of marbles in your back pocket that would make a six-year-old proud!

## THE DANGER OF DEBATE

**Be warned:** There is danger in too much debate. Not only does it waste valuable negotiating time, but if you have a weak position, you could be setting yourself up for a fall. The longer you spend in discussion, the greater the opportunity for the other party to find out that you are on shaky ground.

Let's say you are selling something – cars, watches, software, hardware, cooking appliances, whatever – and you are aware that a new model of your product is going to be launched some time in the near future. Your company is not going to let you off work (or your sales target) until the new product becomes available, so you have no choice but to continue selling the current one. The longer you spend chatting to any potential buyer, the greater the chance that they will question you about future offerings. Even though you might not know the details, any disclosure on your part may result in them wanting to delay their purchasing decision. You need to meet, put your proposal on the table, give the buyer a good reason for buying (perhaps a really attractive offer) and leave with the order. This is not the time to use too much persuasion or to get into a detailed conversation.

Another debate that could turn dangerous would be when you agree with the other party's position. Imagine that your company has failed to deliver something to a customer that was really important to them. Your company blames someone else for the mistake, but you believe your company was actually in the wrong. The longer your conversation with the customer, the more likely he is to discover that you think he's right. He will probably use this information as leverage for being paid compensation or whatever he may want from your organisation. Again, present your proposal to rectify the problem, give the customer a good reason to accept the proposal, and leave with the agreement.

Both of these examples are from real life (names not disclosed to protect the guilty), but there are plenty of cases I could cite where too much debate damaged one party's position. Make your proposal, get it agreed – and get the hell out of Dodge.

Another situation in which the 'get in, get signature, get out' rule needs to apply is when you are going round and round in square circles. Have you ever heard the tale of the Oozlum bird? A legendary creature from British and Australian folklore, the Oozlum bird flies around in ever-decreasing circles until it eventually disappears up its own anal orifice, as my colleague David Black is wont to say. Too much discussion can lead to a deal disappearing up its own backside. If you find that you are getting that feeling of déjà vu … déjà vu … déjà vu …, it's time to summarise and state the next step – and then make sure the discussion moves on.

Here are a few more situations in which you need to limit or control debate as much as possible and focus instead on trading, closing the deal and moving on.

1. Time constraints: Debate consumes time without necessarily moving the deal forward. Negotiation is usually what closes the deal.
2. Conflict or tension arises: The more time spent in debate, the greater the opportunity for conflict to develop or escalate. Summaries are objective and thus help to reduce tension. And use trading – it focuses people on what they will gain rather than on arguing.
3. Too many opinions are expressed: This often allows competitive behaviour and emotion to enter the discussions, which, in turn, can result in conflict. You can't negotiate an argument; you can only win an argument – which is actually win-lose.
4. You are dealing with hostile or abusive people: Those wanting to make or score points prefer debate to negotiation, as it provides them with the ideal platform from which to launch the abuse. Summaries and trading are the best options with these clowns.

So, you need to be able to distinguish good debate from bad debate ('good' moves the discussion forward, while 'bad' launches the Oozlum bird). When you find yourself in a conversation that is going nowhere fast, it is best to:

- summarise; then
- call a time-out to reconsider your position, or postpone and reschedule the meeting; then
- meet again and stick to negotiating!

## A LESSON IN COMMUNICATION

This joke is a favourite of Paul Keates, a colleague of mine. He thinks it's hilarious. Most men would, I fear. The moral of the story is this: Get all the information you can before exposing your hand – or anything else, for that matter.

> A man is getting into the shower just as his wife is finishing up her shower, when the doorbell rings. The wife quickly wraps herself in a towel and runs downstairs. When she opens the door, there stands Bob, the next-door neighbour.
>
> Before she can say a word, Bob says, 'I'll give you $800 to drop that towel.' After thinking for a moment, the woman drops her towel and stands naked in front of Bob. A few seconds later Bob hands her $800 and leaves.
>
> The woman wraps up in the towel and goes back upstairs. When she gets to the bathroom, her husband asks, 'Who was that?'
>
> 'It was Bob from next door,' she replies.
>
> 'Great,' says the husband, 'did he say anything about the $800 he owes me?'

Original source unknown

## Chapter 5

## THE POWER AND THE GLORY

> 'Men are taught to apologise for their weaknesses, women for their strengths.'
> – Lois Wyse (American author and columnist; 1926–2007)

We have a few more fabulous topics into which we will sink our teeth before we get to the 'how' of negotiation and before you become, ta-dah, a bona fide deal diva! The last bite (save for one more tiny munch) of the dealmaker definition that we need to take is that of 'power':

> Dealmaker: A person skilled in using instinct, processes and expertise in primarily negotiation, selling and communication, and <u>able to leverage or adjust the balance of power</u> to bring closure to transactions that usually benefit all parties.
>
> © The Dealmaker Programmes Company

It's all good and well to have power, but power for its own sake is not what we are trying to achieve here. In the context of dealmaking, it is how we create and use power in a negotiation that makes all the difference.

Roseanne Barr (*American comedienne and actor; 1952–*) infamously said, 'The thing women have got to learn is that nobody gives you power. You just take it.'

Now, not everyone is as bold and brazen as Ms Barr, but the first step in creating power is to *decide what you want*. Women are often accused of not knowing what they want, yet when they do pursue their objectives, they are called gold-diggers or ball-busters or something similarly ridiculous.

As we discussed in Chapter 1, women have been expected to perform certain tasks and behave in a certain way since time immemorial. Women have bowed and scraped for millennia, and now that they are standing up for themselves, they get tarred with epithets such as feminists, bitches, hussies, sirens and she-devils. The idiot brigade would like to tag us all 'Submissive Womenfolk'. We need to rebel. We need to get out there and communicate our expectations. This does not mean, however, that we should not be true to who we are as individuals – we just need to find our inner Roseanne. (More about your character when we delve into behaviour in the next chapter.)

By the by, if you are thinking that I am delusional and that times really have changed and that men are happy for women to pursue what they want, consider this statement by evangelist Marion Gordon 'Pat' Robertson: 'The feminist agenda is not about equal rights for women. It is about a socialist, anti-family political movement that encourages women to leave their husbands, kill their children, practice witchcraft, destroy capitalism, and become lesbians.' When do you think this was written? Three hundred years ago? No, it was written in 1992, when this *[insert your own very rude word here for this asshole]* was apparently raising funds for the Republican Party in America.

Over and above knowing what you want, it is possible to make power from very little. The problem is that most women don't know where to start looking. It might be right before their eyes, but they just can't see it. It's a bit like me and cooking. I hate cooking. My cooking talents extend to throwing frozen peas and tinned sweetcorn in with two-minute noodles. I can look in the cupboard and see nothing to eat. My husband will look in the same cupboard and produce a gourmet meal.

Pretend, for the moment, that you look inside your pantry and all you can find are some dog biscuits and a jar of olives. Before you declare that the pantry is bare, you need to decide whether you want to feed the dog or cater for a cocktail party. It's amazing how many people won't even know that they are eating dog biscuits.

### The perfect chicken recipe

I've just confessed that I hate cooking. My terribly helpful sister, Shelley Lotriet, sent this recipe to me. She thought it was perfect for someone who is never sure how to tell when poultry is cooked thoroughly without being dried out. Give it a try.

Baked stuffed chicken

- 3–3.5 kg chicken
- 1 cup melted butter
- 1 cup stuffing
- 1 cup uncooked popcorn
- Salt and pepper to taste

1. Preheat oven to 350 degrees Celsius.
2. Brush chicken well with melted butter, salt and pepper.
3. Fill cavity with stuffing and popcorn.
4. Place in baking pan with the neck end towards the back of the oven.
5. Listen for popping sounds.
6. When the chicken's ass blows the oven door open and the chicken flies across the room, it's done!

Thanks, Shelley.

## CREATING POWER FROM THE ALMOST-EMPTY PANTRY

Earlier in the book I asked you how it was possible for a child, who has virtually no power in a negotiation with an adult, to successfully get what they want. Here's a quick recap of the six ways in which kids find power from a zero base:

1. They tell you what they want.
2. They are infinitely creative.

3. They are infinitely flexible.
4. They do not apply logic to their proposals.
5. They are ruthless traders.
6. They don't care about ego or losing face.

There are lots of ways to make power from next to nothing. Below are the bare bones of what we are going to cover. The bone that will attract the most attention is the one that has the most power potential – planning.
- Getting your negotiating gear engaged.
- The power of planning – information, questions, listening.
- The power of carrots.
- Who really, really needs the deal?
- Perceptions of you – your personal authority, legitimacy, knowledge, credibility and appearance.
- Language and word power.

### GETTING YOUR NEGOTIATING GEAR ENGAGED

I have mentioned negotiating, or trading, or giving to get, or quid pro quo, or 'if you don't ask, you don't get', or 'ask and ye shall receive' a squillion times. To be a powerful dealmaker you must embrace the principle of 'give to get' – and embrace it as if you were a child (look *again* at the six strengths of a child negotiator). The childlike mindset of being flexible and creative is critical when you are battling to establish your power in a deal, or when you are in a genuinely weak position. The weaker your position, the more you will need to focus on trading – offering incentives and variables (carrots and slices of carrot). To do this, you must know what you want, the maximum with which you can open the negotiation and the minimum that you will accept. This is covered in detail in the 'how' section of the book.

Back to power: there is inherent power in the trading process, and trading is driven by proposals. To be a powerful dealmaker, you need to make and respond to proposals – and this means having a lot more than one or two carrots and a few marbles with which to negotiate. The skilled dealmaker will always come to the table with lots and lots of variables (or marbles), and will be prepared to trade them. Don't shy away from making trading-based proposals – it is one of the most effective tools you can use to gain, and keep, control of the dealmaking process.

The trick, of course, is to develop a *long* list of marbles. This will mean that you need to sit down and have a quiet little 'marble brainstorming session'. Even skilled negotiators can struggle to think up variables on the spot, so preparing them in advance is a must. There are thirty-seven benefits on the list I developed that one can negotiate along with a salary package. This needs to be the norm, not the exception.

## THE POWER OF PLANNING

> 'Make no small plans for they have no power to stir the soul.'
> – Niccolo Machiavelli
> (Italian diplomat and politician; 1469–1527)

This brings us to planning, and planning is where we are going to spend the most time relative to creating power.

A friend of mine who is one of the highest-earning salespeople in the country (no names mentioned to protect him from the headhunters) reminds everyone, all the time, to the point of irritation in fact – sorry Greg – about the 'Six **P**s of Planning': 'Proper Planning Prevents Piss-Poor Performance'.

Planning is a huge subject, but, within the framework of power, planning needs to be your starting point. If you fail to plan the negotiation, don't be surprised when – not if – you end up with a piss-poor deal.

Gary Player (*South African world-class golfer; 1935–*) is attributed with saying: 'The harder I practise, the luckier I get.' The same will apply to your power base in a deal. The more you plan, the more you will get what you want. Every successful businessperson to whom I have ever spoken has always been at pains to point out that not only do they work hard and make sacrifices, but they also spend an inordinate amount of time planning – which includes learning, reading and researching.

There are three elements we are going to look at from a 'planning your power' perspective. They are information, questions and listening.

## The power of information

You must live in a cave if you have never heard the saying 'information is power'. In fact, I know you have heard it, because I mentioned it when we spoke about debate in the section on communication. What I said is that it's not actually information that is power; it's how you *use* the information that gives you the power. Information simply for information's sake is pointless – determine what you know, what you need to know, and then fill in the gaps.

There are many ways to gather information, so when it comes to doing your homework, saying, 'I couldn't find what I was looking for' is pathetic. Here are a few ideas: the internet (hurrah for Google!), websites, magazines, periodicals, newspapers, books, libraries, specialist clubs, professional associations, annual reports, analyst reports, newsletters, company notice boards … Have a look at www.noodletools.com/debbie/literacies/information/5locate/adviceengine.html for an incredible list of ideas. Of course, the most powerful way to obtain information is to ask the person concerned directly, but more about this when we cover the power of questions.

When you use information to increase your power, you need to bear in mind the following *four important points* on how to exploit the information.

## FOUR RULES FOR USING AND ABUSING INFORMATION
### 1. Don't invent 'facts'

As I've said before, if you fabricate anything and the other person finds out, your credibility and negotiating power go to hell in a handcart. Being caught out in a lie also makes the other party mistrust everything else you have said or will say. I suspect people lie because they think that it will increase their power in a negotiation. Lying may give you a short-term advantage – if you don't get found out – but, in the long term, 'the truth will out'.

It does not matter if you are lying to someone else or to yourself, nobody respects a liar. Ask Joost. Ask Bill Clinton.

## 2. Use information to 'set expectations'

Using information intelligently is a carefully calculated source of power. We already know that when you set expectations, you get the other person to think in the way *you* want them to think. You can pass information to them directly, or drop little clues. You can tell them what you want, signal how flexible you are, or state where you are and where you are not negotiable. Setting expectations can range from making brazen Roseanne-style proposals to dropping subtle hints and suggestions. You need to choose whatever will work best for you to direct the other party's thinking.

If using information properly gives you power, you should also provide the other person with the data that substantiates or helps your case. This, of course, means carefully planning your disclosures.

It is within your power to choose consciously how you want to set expectations. To do this effectively, you will need to think about *what* you are saying and *how* you are saying it. Have a quick reread of conscious and unconscious verbal communication.

## 3. There is an art to disclosing or withholding information

The best way to illustrate what I mean is with an example. As I have mentioned, my yummy hubby Simon loves big, fast motorbikes. When he wanted to buy a Ducati 996 (before you ask, I would rather stick needles in my eyes than ride on the back), it took him ages to find it, then ages to decide if it was the one he really wanted, then even longer to figure out the most he should pay for it. (More about Simon's unique method of making decisions later – see the story of the Land Cruiser.)

Anyhow, by now he knows the salesperson by name. Pinky, I think it was. Every time he goes in to the Ducati shop to look at the bike, they have coffee. Eventually Simon makes Pinky an offer of R105 000 (for the bike!). Pinky says nothing, but sashays into the office and returns with a piece of paper showing that the shop had bought the bike for R100 000. Was this good or bad disclosure on Pinky's part? I bet you think that it was *bad* for her to show Simon the profit margin. Not so. Pinky had showed Simon that the shop would make only R5 000 on his offer, but they still had to factor in the financial cost of holding the bike as stock. Simon had to up his offer quite a bit to make the deal.

If, however, the paper Pinky had shown Simon reflected a purchase price of R80 000, she would have been dead in the water in that negotiation. *Information is power*, but you need to use it to your best advantage.

## 4. Diverting attention from information that you do not want to disclose

In the section on communication, I asked you if you knew how to divert attention away from sensitive subjects, or from questions you would rather not answer. Simply blocking questions is considered obstructive and will not necessarily increase your power. You must, of course, know what information you do *not* want to disclose – and this requires thought and planning.

If you suspect someone will abuse the information they want from you, simply saying 'I am not prepared to answer that' gives far too many clues to the asker about the possible answer. Here's how it works. If someone asks you for your profit margin on an item and you say 'I am not prepared to disclose that', they will assume that your profit is high, because if it was low, you would probably share the information.

So, how do you avoid disclosing information you don't want to give? If you are thinking, 'Ask them a question,' you are on the money, girl. The best 'deflection' questions you can ask are:
- Why do you want to know that?
- Why is this information important to you?
- What is your reason for asking the question?
- Can I ask *you* a question? What …? (Ask them a personal question.)

The irony is that people are flattered when you are interested in them – and it is the easiest way to distract someone away from the information they wanted from you.

## The power of questions

What is the best and most reliable way of obtaining information? Asking the person concerned for the information directly. It's that simple. In a conversation, two-thirds of the time should be spent listening, and half of the time that's left (work out those numbers, woman – it's a sixth!) should be spent asking questions. People actually like to be asked questions – especially about themselves.

There are a few guidelines to follow in order to extract power from questions. For example, firing a string of question marks at the other person is pretty pointless. Another example: never underestimate the power of face-to-face questioning. When you ask the relevant person for the information directly, you have the opportunity to aurally *and* visually pick up the nuances and subtleties that accompany their answers – the 'clues', in other words. As you know, effective communication is about choosing your words carefully, picking up the clues, observing, and listening to your intuition.

Here are *three fabulous ways* to maximise the use of questions to increase your power.

## THREE WAYS TO MAKE THE MOST OF YOUR QUESTIONS
### 1. The quality of your questions determines the quality of the answers

Poor-quality questions result in unclear and vague answers. Quality questions seldom happen by chance or on the spur of the moment – they are prepared in advance. You should, in fact, prepare as many of your questions as possible beforehand.

If you want an example to illustrate how powerful the quality of a question can be, think Peter Sellers in *The Pink Panther Strikes Again*. In this particular movie, Peter Sellers' character, the bumbling Chief Inspector Jacques Clouseau, is standing at the reception desk of a hotel when he sees a dog lying next to the front door. 'Does your dog bite?' asks Inspector Clouseau of the man at the desk (which, in his ridiculous French accent, comes out as, 'Does yer derg bite?'). The man answers no. Inspector Clouseau bends down to pat the dog, which promptly growls and sinks its teeth into him. Shocked, he exclaims, 'I thought that you said your derg does not bite!'

'*Oui*,' responds the man, 'but that is not my dog.'

Anthony Robbins (*American author and motivator; 1960 –*) says that 'Successful people ask better questions, and as a result, they get better answers.' The power is in the quality, not the quantity.

## 2. Never feel uncomfortable asking for information – even sensitive information

There are three reasons why people don't ask for information:

i. *They are afraid the answer might not be what they want to hear.*

In negotiation, and in establishing power, it is essential to get the answers – even if you are concerned as to what they might be. Don't you think it's better to know early on in the proceedings if there is going to be a problem? At least then you still have time left to address the issues.

ii. *They can't think of the right questions to ask.*

The argument I generally hear from people who do not prepare questions before a negotiation is that one never knows where the discussions will go. This is true, but nobody (hopefully) meets without knowing what they are going to discuss. If you have an agenda, or even just the topic for the meeting, you have enough information with which to prepare questions. As I've said before, there are not that many people who are clever enough to think up everything on the spot.

iii. *They are too busy talking to think about asking for information.*

Some people just *love* the sound of their own voices. But a conversation is a dialogue, not a Shakespearian monologue. The best negotiators I know – even the very egocentric ones – always make sure that they get the information they need. And how do they do this? They ask questions. Duh!

### Sensitive information

There is a certain arrogance in not wanting to ask for sensitive information. We decide – on behalf of the person we are going to quiz – whether he will be comfortable or not answering a question *we* think is sensitive. Give him the option, for heaven's sake, of making his own decision.

I mentioned in *Work Diva* that the coaches who deliver The Dealmaker™ programmes have great fun thinking up the most outrageous questions they can ask the delegates on the courses. A favourite is to ask someone – bearing in mind that this person will be answering in front of complete strangers (or, even worse, colleagues) – how many different sexual partners he has had. Can you believe that most people are willing to open their proverbial bedroom doors? People will answer almost any question you ask them if you ask it directly, unexpectedly and without bad intent.

Imagine having the power to ask anyone anything – *and they will answer you?* It's quite easy, actually – and this is detail I did not include in *Work Diva*. The power lies in *how* you ask the question. And here's *how*:

- The question must be crystal clear and not longer than one sentence.
- Use very direct, plain language – do not clarify, expand or explain.
- Ask the question only once.
- Look the person directly in the eye when you ask the question.
- If the person repeats the question to you or rephrases it, just nod once.
- WAIT for the person to answer – do *not* explain, look away, fidget, signal or blink (if possible).
- If you have to wait two minutes, so be it.
- Thank the person for their openness once he or she has answered.
- Do not interrogate the person on the information disclosed. You can come back to it later if necessary.
- Move on to the next subject – one that is not sensitive.

What if this technique fails? The best thing to do if someone refuses to answer – or after *at least* a two-minute wait has produced no answer – is to acknowledge the person's choice not to answer and to move on to a less sensitive question.

**But:** Do not try this at home! If you think your partner, child or whoever is hiding something from you, or lying to you, no matter how you ask the questions, they will not tell you something they do not want you to know. Because, try as you might, I doubt you will ever get the question to be unexpected – which is the key.

The power in this technique is compelling. Why? It's actually to do with the interview*ee*. The answer automatically pops into their head, but it is the pressure of the silence that forces them to spit it out.

In the negotiating context, you owe it to yourself to ask the difficult questions – let the person you are asking decide whether he or she wants to answer or not.

### 3. Interesting people are interested in others

This is one of my pet subjects. Think about the last function you attended where you did not know many people. Try to remember who it was that you found most interesting (not handsome) at the event. I'm pretty sure it will be the person who asked you lots of questions about yourself. People do like to talk about themselves, but again, the power is in the quality of the questions.

Asking, 'So what do you do?' of someone is the social equivalent of finding dog poo on your shoe. If someone asks me this in a social setting, I move on to more interesting ground pronto. It is acceptable in a business context – if somewhat uninspired – because you presumably want to capitalise on the networking opportunities. But really, is this the best that we can do?

People are so much more interesting than their jobs. Make it your business to find out something interesting about every single person you meet from now on. You will find that suddenly everyone wants to know more about *you*. Find out what motivates the person to get up in the morning, what she would do differently with her life if she were suddenly twenty-one again, what pizza topping she would be (read *Quirkology* by Dr Richard Wiseman – the scientist who found that all kids lie – to discover the power in *this* question!), which is her favourite ice-cream flavour ... that sort of thing.

For my organisation's newsletter, we have a list of questions that we can ask the people we are interviewing to help us uncover the unusual things about them. Here are a few examples. Feel free to use any of them!

– What has been the proudest moment of your life?

- Where is the most interesting place you have ever visited? Why?
- What is the most interesting thing you have ever seen? Why?
- Where do you dream about visiting? Why?
- Do you have a 'life list'? What sort of things are on your list?
- Can you tell me one thing that nobody knows about you?
- What is the biggest lie you tell about yourself?
- What is the biggest lie you tell to yourself?
- What would your partner/spouse say are your three greatest abilities?
- If you were a superhero, which one would you be? Why?
- What is the best advice a grandparent ever gave you?
- What is your favourite gadget of the moment?
- If you were president for one day, what law would you put in place? And remove?
- If you could assassinate one person with absolutely no consequences, who would it be? Why?
- If you could choose the president of the entire universe, who would you choose, and why?
- What would you like to be remembered for having achieved in your life?
- If you were given the opportunity to have dinner with one person, alive or dead, who would you choose, and why?

If it has to be about work:
- When you were six, ten and sixteen, what were your dream jobs?
- What was your first job and how much was your paycheck?
- Describe, in one sentence, your current job to a five-year-old.
- What is the best advice a business mentor gave you? Who was the mentor?
- What is the most unusual strategy or technique you have used to get what you want in business?
- In your career, what has been your greatest achievement so far?
- What do you do in your spare time to blow off steam or relax?

Interesting people are interested in others – ask lots of questions and listen to the answers. It makes people feel special, which they are.

### The power of listening

The much-loved wit Will Rogers (*American actor and author; 1879–1935*) came up with two of my favourite sayings about listening: 'Never miss a good chance to shut up,' and, 'Lettin' the cat outta the bag is a whole lot easier 'n puttin' it back in.'

In today's world of me-me-me, go-go-go, the art of listening appears to have been lost. It is not because we are advancing as a species that we now talk about 'active listening' and 'being in the moment'. I believe that because people don't listen any more we are forced to try to find new and interesting ways to encourage them to pay attention.

If you don't listen properly, the communication process goes for a ball of chalk. You can't pick up the clues, you won't get the information you need, you miss the signs of flexibility and you fail to identify what is important to the other party. All of which means your ability to make proposals and negotiate is compromised and you end up paying more for what you want than you needed to pay.

To compound matters, research suggests that the average listener understands and retains only half of a conversation, and this drops to a retention rate of 25 per cent two days after the conversation. The implication is that when we don't (or can't) listen properly, our ability to recall a conversation that took place more than forty-eight hours ago is incomplete and unreliable. This no doubt exacerbates the conflict and tension inherent in difficult discussions.

When you listen, do try to 'be in the moment', as New Age practitioners like to say. Be fully present – listen to the words being used and to their context. Don't think about anything other than what is being said and how it is being said. Listen. Pause. Think. Speak.

Never underestimate the power in being silent. Don't be afraid to carry on listening when nothing is being said. There is *huge* strength in stillness. Don't feel that you need to fill the empty space with words, or that you must ease the tension created by the silence. Keep quiet. Learn to be comfortable with silence. If you can achieve this, you will find that, because *others* are uncomfortable with silence, *they* will start talking – and because what they say will be unrehearsed, out will come all the secrets.

The best possible illustration of the power of silence is what I revealed to you in the point about getting people to answer sensitive questions. As I said then, it is the *pressure of the silence* that makes them reveal what they would never otherwise have told you.

Here follows the 'listening' version of the *Goldilocks and the Three Bears* fairy tale.

> Baby Bear goes downstairs and sits in his small chair at the table. He looks into his small bowl, and it is empty. 'Who's been eating my porridge?' he squeaks.
>
> Papa Bear arrives at the table and sits in his big chair. He looks into his big bowl, and it is also empty. 'Who's been eating my porridge!' he roars.
>
> Momma Bear puts her head through the serving hatch and from the kitchen yells, 'How many times do I have to go through this with you idiots? It was Momma Bear who got up first, it was Momma Bear who woke everyone in the house, it was Momma Bear who made the coffee, it was Momma Bear who unloaded the dishwasher from last night and put everything away, it was Momma Bear who went out in the cold early-morning air to fetch the newspaper, it was Momma Bear who set the damn table, it was Momma Bear who put the friggin' cat out, cleaned the litter box, and filled the cat's water and food dishes, and now that you've decided to drag your sorry bear-asses downstairs and grace Momma Bear's dining room with your grumpy presence, listen and listen good, 'cause I am only going to say this one more time: I HAVEN'T MADE THE #%$@& PORRIDGE YET!'

## THE POWER OF CARROTS

Early on in this chapter I said that there are lots of ways to create power from next to nothing. We have looked primarily at 'The power of planning' – which included information, questions and listening. But now it's time to talk carrots (and I don't mean 'giving someone a carrot' in its colloquial sense).

We have already discussed incentives (or carrots), in considerable detail. Our first exposure to incentives was with the concept presented in the book *Freakonomics* – and the fact that children take to incentives like proverbial ducks to water. The truth is, strength lies in carrots – and not spinach, as Popeye thought.

I have called carrots by lots of other names – incentives, variables, marbles, concessions, demands, offers, hot buttons – but that which we call a carrot, by any name, is still a great source of power (to misquote Shakespeare). When we get to the 'how' of negotiating, particularly defining the ballpark, you will learn that there are two types of carrots: *key* issues (big carrots) and *secondary* issues (marbles, small carrots or carrot slices). As I have already said countless times, you need to think up lots and lots of carrots *as part of your planning* to give you dealmaking power.

The beauty of carrots is that when you find yourself with your back to the wall, all you have to do is produce carrots that the other side will find irresistible. It's the ultimate value proposition. The whole essence of getting what you want in a negotiation is to give the other side what *they* want. Give them the carrots that *they* want – not the ones you *want* to give away – and you have your ultimate source of power. You trade your key issues for big carrots from them, and you use the small carrots to even out the deal. Remember the thirty-seven fringe benefits to get the total salary package you wanted? You can also bunch lots of small carrots together in exchange for a big carrot, but be sure you are getting value for value.

When you trade carrots, here is how *your* side of the negotiating conversation goes:

'If you give me the fifty purple carrots I want, I can give you three dozen bunches of orange carrots.'

'Okay, if you don't want to give me the purple carrots, you can give me sixty of the pink ones, but then you only get two dozen bunches in return.'

'Well, if you're only prepared to give me forty pink carrots, I will need three carving knives too.'

'If you are not happy with the knives, I need forty pink carrots, six forks, two partridges *and* a pear tree in exchange for the two bunches of orange carrots I will give you.'

Get the picture?

The more incentives you can find to entice the other party, the more interest he will have in doing the deal with you, and the greater your power. Remember that *dis*incentives are a form of negative carrot.

(Just out of interest, did you know that there is a World Carrot Museum? See www.carrotmuseum.co.uk. It has nothing to do with negotiating.)

## WHO REALLY, REALLY NEEDS THE DEAL?

What does it say about your power if you can't walk away? Another central element in determining power is to establish which side needs the deal more. It obviously stands to reason that the side that really needs the deal is in the weaker position. Sometimes there is little you can do to change this situation, so if it is *you* that needs the deal more than the other party, you need to spend as much time as possible investigating the ways in which you can improve your power. How do you make gold soup? Use twenty-two carrots (joke – got that one from the World Carrot Museum).

When it comes to monopolies, you often have no choice but to do business with them. They have all the power, so they dictate the terms. Monopolies are renowned for holding their customers – and business partners – to ransom. It's the same with sole suppliers – if you don't want to work with them, tough. Their power lies in the fact that you can't get the product anywhere else. What happens to the monopolies and sole suppliers when the tide turns and competition enters the market? Do you remember Telkom before Neotel? Can you imagine what we would be paying in cellphone charges if there were only one provider?

The opposite of a monopoly is the person who can choose from any number of suppliers and then proceeds to play one supplier off against the others in order to drive down prices or improve the terms of a deal. A graduate of one of The Dealmaker™ programmes decided to play this game with low-cost insurance providers. She managed to secure an outrageously low premium in the end.

This is very similar to being married versus being single. A marriage is a monopoly – a sole-supplier arrangement. In a marriage, you either have fun with your spouse, or you are celibate (presuming you are monogamous). The single person, however, gets to choose with whom she wants to have fun, so she can (if she wants) trade one competitor off against another to find the best 'deal'. But situations change, and the singleton may decide that she is sick of all the different suppliers so she enters into a long-term relationship with the supplier she likes the most – and they get married. A married person, on the other hand, may get tired of being monopolised and go off in search of other suppliers. (Read the divine Tess Stimson's divine book *Beat the Bitch* if you want to stray-proof your marriage or long-term relationship. Be warned, however: it is not for the prudish.)

To increase your power, find out whether you are able to use sole supply or competition to improve your deal. Even though it may not seem fair, both companies and individuals use it every single day to strengthen their positions of power.

## PERCEPTIONS OF YOU

Your personal authority, legitimacy, knowledge, credibility and appearance all influence your power, believe it or not.

The more authority and legitimacy you have – as recognised by the other party – the greater your power. Perception is reality, so if the other party does not see you as having the necessary authority or legitimacy, your position is immediately undermined. This, in turn, reduces your power. Why do you think the people formerly known as 'sales representatives' are now called 'account executives'? The change was first made to elevate the profile of the individual – to give the impression that their authority was that of an executive. People quickly caught on to that one, but I think the change was good. Not all salespeople are bottom dwellers. The salespeople I know deserve to be treated with respect – many of them earn more than their managing directors.

Two further factors influencing personal power are credibility and appearance. If you don't look and act the part, or if your credentials are not up to scratch, your power is compromised. It may be acceptable for Sir Richard Branson to look like the Wild Man of Borneo, but until you have his authority and legitimacy, you need to make the very most of your physical appearance. You are what you wear. You are how you look. Unfortunately this is the nature of human nature. If you want to be taken seriously, send out the message via your appearance as much as you do via your behaviour and hard work. And don't think that this does not apply to homemakers too! If you want to buy a house, say, or discuss your child's progress at the parent–teachers' meeting, people need to take you seriously – dress accordingly.

As for credibility, can you see the connection between power and self-promotion? Do not be too modest in establishing your credentials – be proud of your achievements – and don't be self-effacing when establishing your credibility during negotiations.

The most effective and positive way in which you can impart your personal authority, legitimacy, credibility and appearance is through your knowledge. People respect someone who knows of that which she speaks. They respect people who take the time and trouble to get the appropriate information. They admire people who have invested in themselves to improve their expertise. Your knowledge is well within your power to improve.

In *Work Diva*, I listed *ten sure-fire ways* with which to establish credibility and earn respect. I have included an edited list below, as omitting these issues in the quest to increase your personal power would be remiss of me.

## TEN SURE-FIRE WAYS WITH WHICH TO INCREASE YOUR PERSONAL POWER

### 1. Under-promise and over-deliver

Don't disappoint others by saying you will deliver something to them on a certain date or to a certain quality and then deliver late or less than they were expecting. Even if you do the very best that you can, delivering late or less always puts you in a bad light. Rather set the right expectations of what and by when you can deliver at the *beginning* of a project, and then pleasantly surprise those around you by exceeding expectations.

## 2. Get things done

I call one of the women with whom my organisation works 'The Girl Who Gets Things Done'. If she says she will do something, she does it. She sees assignments through to completion, regardless of the challenges and obstacles she encounters. Too many people simply give up when the going gets tough and then justify their failure to finish the job with a myriad excuses. There is a big difference between knowing when it's a good time to throw in the towel and throwing it in just because the going got too tough.

## 3. Be consistent

People want predictability – they do not want someone who can be charming one minute but then flies into a rage or a sulk the next. Divas on whom people can depend, and not those who are up one minute and down the next, get promoted. We all have our moods, but the more you can regulate yours, the bigger the favour you'll be doing yourself. It *is* possible to control *your* behaviour, even if you can't control the behaviour of others. (More about behaviour in the next chapter.)

## 4. Work hard and work smart

Working hard is not enough. You need to work hard *and* smart *at the same time*. But what does 'working smart' mean? It's knowing how to prioritise, where best to invest your energy and resources, understanding the difference between what's urgent and what's important, and being able to delegate appropriately. If you're not sure how to work smarter, ask someone you admire to mentor or guide you.

## 5. Say what you mean and mean what you say

Get to the point and choose your words carefully. Nothing is more irritating than someone who dithers or uses fifty words when fifteen would suffice. This does not mean that you shouldn't explain things properly; it just means that you need to think about what you want to say and how to say it, and then say it. Keep your communication – whether oral or written – clear, concise and honest. And say what you mean – don't be a duplicitous, deceitful clever dick. People need to be able to rely on what you say, so don't say things you don't mean.

## 6. Keep your word
As part of building respect, people need to be able to trust you at your word. If you make a promise to do something or be somewhere, make sure that that is what you do, even if it means you are inconvenienced. People put huge store by the promises of others, so do everything in your power to be known as someone upon whom others can depend – someone who keeps her promises.

## 7. Tell the truth, despite the consequences
Where do you draw the line? Do you convince yourself that it's okay to tell a little white lie to spare someone's feelings? What if it's a big lie to protect someone you love? I try always to tell the truth (I can't remember the lies, so I would get easily caught out), but where the truth will hurt someone, I choose my words very carefully. As I've said before, nobody respects a liar.

## 8. Take responsibility
This operates on two levels – accepting responsibility in the form of the duties or roles expected of you, and then taking responsibility for your actions. In accepting responsibility, you will be given the credit if the project is a success, but you will also carry the blame if it all goes horribly wrong. You can have both, or neither. Your choice. Only a victim tries get away with taking one (you can guess which one) without the other.

## 9. Don't be afraid to make the difficult decisions
Many people battle with making decisions, never mind making the unpopular ones. Decision-making, like most other skills and talents, can be learnt. But *how* does one make a difficult or unpopular decision? It comes back to the truth: be true to yourself. You owe it to yourself, and to the people who will be impacted by your decision, to think through all the options, consequences and outcomes. If you

then make a decision that you believe in your heart to be the right one, you will be okay. Even if it all goes wrong, you will be able to justify (even if only to yourself) the basis of your decision. Be brave. One Franklin P. Jones (*identity not confirmed*) says, 'Bravery is being the only one who knows you are afraid.'

## 10. Treat others with respect

Do you show respect to other people? Think about how you treat the waiters in a restaurant or the cleaners in a public loo. Many people try to elevate themselves by treating others badly, but all they're really showing is that they lack manners and grace. Grace is the ability to show someone respect without being servile or obsequious. Grace comes across as good manners. For example, being on time illustrates not only professionalism but also respect for the other person's time. If you treat others with disrespect, don't be surprised when you are treated in the same contemptuous manner.

There is no substitute for commitment and hard work – in dealmaking, effort is rewarded with results. The time you invest in planning, obtaining information, preparing questions, selecting and briefing your team, practising your opening positions, etc., will always pay dividends. This, of course, means hard work.

## LANGUAGE AND WORD POWER

In the chapter on communication I banged on about the importance of language and the words we use in dealmaking, particularly in negotiation. Suffice to say that if there is only one word I want you to remember, it is the word '*if*'. '*If*' suggests conditions; 'if' suggests trading; 'if' is the panacea of all power in negotiation. For professional dealmakers, it is the most powerful word in the dealmaking world. In fact, I believe 'if' to be the meaning of l*if*e!

## NEGOTIATING FROM A WEAK POSITION

When you are negotiating from a position of weakness, you need to do as much as you possibly can to increase your power. You need to focus on:

- Getting your negotiating gear engaged – don't be afraid to trade.
- The power of planning – information, questions, listening, silence. Time invested in planning always, always, always pays dividends.
- The power of carrots – the more you have to ask for and to offer, the merrier.
- Understanding which side really, really needs the deal.
- Personal power – your authority, legitimacy, credibility and appearance are important, but none is as important as your knowledge.
- Language and word power – if, if, if …

Any improvement in your power is going to help you when it comes to negotiating the deal. Over and above these key power ingredients that you need to find in your pantry, here are six more ideas to try:

1. Do not multitask when you plan for the negotiation or deal. Give your preparation time your complete and undivided attention. Remember the impact of multitasking on those IQ points!
2. To help you focus when you are planning, play some light classical music in the background. Research shows that classical music, particularly Baroque (i.e. Mozart, Vivaldi, Albinoni, Handel, et al.) enhances learning and memory, improves creativity and clarity, stimulates concentration and comprehension, and is excellent for your unborn child, too. You can read more about this in *The Mozart Effect: Tapping the Power of Music to Heal the Body, Strengthen the Mind, and Unlock the Creative Spirit* by Don Campbell.
3. Use a SWOT analysis (Strengths, Weaknesses, Opportunities, Threats) to assess and improve your position and your power.
4. Recognise that there is huge power in making proposals – it is the proposal on the table, full of juicy carrots, that drives the deal forward (more about this when we talk about the 'how').
5. Beware of too much debate when you are in a weak position. Avoid arguments and stick to trading when the other party holds more card than you.
6. Stay emotionally detached – do *not* let the deal get personal.

DEAL *Diva*

By now you may be thinking that power can be used to gain an unfair advantage. You've got it! When you are negotiating, always check what you are doing to improve your position of power. If you do not use the power available to you, you will not maximise your deal. No skilled dealmaker allows this to happen.

Good luck with adjusting your power. It is yours to change.

## DON'T MESS WITH A DIVA

Here is a story to illustrate the power that comes from learning, reading and researching.

> One morning the husband returns after several hours of fishing and decides to take a nap. Although not familiar with the lake, the wife decides to take the boat out. She motors off a short distance, anchors and starts reading her book.
>
> Along comes a game warden in his boat. He pulls up alongside the woman and says, 'Good morning, ma'am. What are you doing?'
>
> 'Reading a book,' she replies, thinking it's obvious.
>
> 'You're in a restricted fishing area,' he informs her.
>
> 'I'm sorry, officer, but I'm not fishing. I'm reading.'
>
> 'Yes, but you have all the equipment. For all I know you could start at any moment. I'll have to take you in and write you up.'
>
> 'If you do that, I'll have to charge you with sexual assault,' says the woman.
>
> 'But I haven't touched you,' says the game warden.
>
> 'That's true, but you have all the equipment. For all I know you could start at any moment.'
>
> 'Have a nice day, ma'am,' and off the game warden went.
>
> The moral of the story? Never argue with a woman who reads. It's likely she can also think.
>
> Original author unknown

## Chapter 6

## BEING THE DIVA YOU ARE MEANT TO BE

> 'When a woman behaves like a man, why doesn't she behave like a nice man?'
> – Dame Edith Evans (British stage actress; 1888–1976)

Yahoo! We are nearly finished eating that elephant-sized dealmaker definition – only the minuscule bit about closing left to go, which we will discuss when we get to the 'how' section. For now, let's get back to talking about *you* and the fabulous individual diva that you are – and understanding more about what makes you tick, and how your behaviour impacts your personal power and value.

One of the questions I am frequently asked about dealmaking is: 'What role does personality play in getting the deal I want?' In my book *Work Diva*, I did discuss personality styles, but for those of you who haven't yet had the chance to read it, I am going to answer the question in detail again. This time, though, I will place specific emphasis on behaviour in the context of dealmaking, and particularly negotiating.

In order to understand the impact of personality type – or, more correctly, behavioural style – on a deal, it is necessary to 'define' the main character types. I've put the word 'define' in quotation marks because we all know that people can't really be boxed into convenient categories. However, to make the complex subject of personality – or behaviour – more manageable, it is important to apply some broad system of categorisation.

The most common tool used to do this is the DISC behavioural model developed in the 1920s by Dr William Moulton Marston (*American psychologist and feminist theorist; 1893–1947*). The fact that so many people have copied or modified the original work of Dr Marston suggests that there must be merit in his classification system. In Dr Marston's system, the 'D' stands for 'Drive', the 'I' for 'Influence', the 'S' for 'Steadiness' and the 'C' for 'Compliance'.

## DETERMINING THE STYLES

If you have done a 'personality types', 'social styles' or any similar kind of profiling course, you will know that there are two axes along which a person's behaviour is generally measured. Dr Marston defined the first axis as 'Assert vs Yield'. This axis is also referred to as:
- A-Type vs B-Type.
- Competitive vs Cooperative.
- Tense vs Easy-going.
- Dominant vs Passive.

For the purposes of dealmaking – which includes a person's selling, negotiating and communication styles – I tend to describe this axis as 'Aggressive vs Agreeable'.

The second axis identified by Dr Marston is the 'Antagonized by vs Allied with' range. This axis is alternatively known as:
- Extravert vs Introvert.
- Impulsive vs Considered.
- Warm vs Cool.
- Spontaneous vs Self-controlled.

Relative to dealmaking, I prefer to use the words 'Sceptical vs Receptive' to describe this axis.

When plotted as one vertical and one horizontal axis crossing each other in the middle, the two axes form four quadrants, or blocks. In a diagram, they look like this:

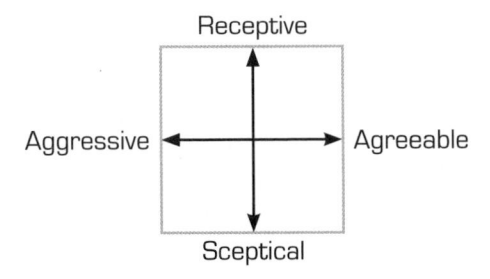

```
              Receptive
                 ↑
    Aggressive ←─┼─→ Agreeable
                 ↓
              Sceptical
```

Each of the four quadrants is then labelled, typically with a word that describes the behaviour defined by that quadrant: for example, a person falling into quadrant 1 (i.e. the Receptive/Aggressive quadrant) is commonly referred to as an 'Expressive', or something similar. A person in quadrant 2 (Receptive/Agreeable) is usually called an 'Amiable'. Collectively, the Expressives and Amiables are the 'warm' people.

Quadrant 3 is Aggressive/Sceptical and the person is known as a 'Driver', while the Agreeable/Sceptical individual of quadrant 4 is an 'Analytical'. These are the 'cool' people.

Grouping the Expressives and Drivers together will give you the 'A-Type' personality, whereas the Amiables and Analyticals are 'B-Type' people.

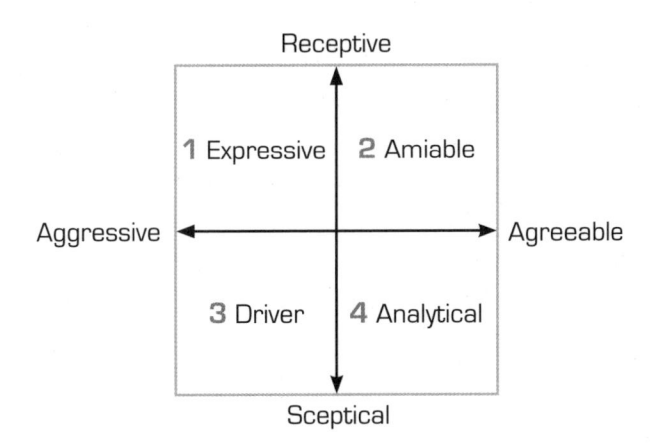

```
                    Receptive
                       ↑
              1 Expressive │ 2 Amiable
                           │
   Aggressive ←────────────┼────────────→ Agreeable
                           │
              3 Driver     │ 4 Analytical
                       ↓
                    Sceptical
```

You may have read Florence Littauer's book *Personality Plus: How to Understand Others by Understanding Yourself.* (If you haven't read *Personality Plus*, it is one of the better books on the subject of understanding different personalities.) If you have, here is how the styles descriptors above compare to those of Ms Littauer:
- Expressive = Sanguine (popular)
- Amiable = Phlegmatic (peaceful)
- Driver = Choleric (powerful)
- Analytical = Melancholy (perfect)

The purpose of these categories is not to pigeonhole people – it is to 'help us make sense of the factors that govern individual social behaviour' (which is another way of saying *understanding what makes different types of people tick*). There is obviously far more theory underlying an intricate concept of this nature, but for our purposes, simple is sufficient.

Which behavioural style are you? Try to figure it out before we go any further. Are you Aggressive or Agreeable? Choose one word. How about Receptive or Sceptical? Again, select only one word. Selecting a word on each axis will identify the quadrant that best describes your *general* behaviour. (A little about *un*general behaviour later.)

And the relevance of the behavioural styles in dealmaking? When meeting a person for the first time, you can try to figure out into which quadrant he would fit – and the majority of the time you'd be on the money. Of course, if you are already familiar with someone, you will have a pretty good idea as to which behavioural style best describes him. Once you have determined the person's quadrant or style, you can then decide how best to deal with him.

When you are negotiating or trading, the most important axis is the Aggressive vs Agreeable alignment. People who are Aggressive (A-Type) are inclined to be competitive, decisive, domineering and distributive. These characteristics increase the tension and the potential for deadlock in a negotiation. The Agreeable people (B-Type) are typically passive, easy-going, cooperative and collaborative, which can mean less confrontation but also fewer decisions. As you can see, neither type is all good or all bad – an expert negotiator will happily shift between both styles in a dealmaking situation, using the one that is most appropriate to the other personalities, the environment and the desired outcome.

## DESCRIBING THE DIFFERENT STYLES

Here are a few guidelines relative to the four quadrants that will help you to recognise the differences between the types and assist you in interacting with them.

### Expressives (Quadrant 1)

*The Director and Ms Mind Changer*

If Expressives were birds, they would be peacocks. If they were animals, they'd be lions.

Expressives are generally confident, sociable, enthusiastic, energetic, impulsive, creative, charming, persuasive, supportive, flighty, manipulative, vague, competitive, undisciplined and tend to overreact – to name but a few of their positive and negative traits.

Their saying of choice is: 'Show me the big picture.' (Remember Cuba Gooding Jr shouting, 'Show me the money!' in the film *Jerry Maguire*? A classic Expressive.)

When negotiating with an Expressive – who is Receptive yet Aggressive – you need to keep the meeting light to avoid confrontation and ensure that the proposals you make hold their interest. Expressives want to be excited by the master plan, not bored with minute details – and they do bore easily. As they are 'expressive', you will know where you stand very quickly. These are enthusiastic people who will often show a positive reaction to your proposal, but they also tend to change their minds.

Remember that Expressives are Aggressive, so they can get nasty if you push or irritate them. The best way to deal with an Expressive is to excite them with what they will get out of the deal and then go for the close. Tie the agreed deal down in writing as soon as you can.

The opposite behavioural style to an Expressive is an Analytical, so sending an Analytical to negotiate with an Expressive is not always the most sensible strategy.

If *you* are the Expressive, people will gravitate towards you, because you are charismatic and engaging. However, because of your love of showmanship, others may not take you seriously. Also, watch that ego!

### Amiables (Quadrant 2)
*Mrs Santa Claus and Helpful Hilda*
Amiables are the doves of the bird world and the giraffes of the animal kingdom.

They are friendly, kind, people-orientated, sympathetic, considerate, willing, supportive, dependable, respectful, conflict-averse, unplanned, indecisive, often feel threatened and are easily intimidated.

Amiables are most likely to say, 'If that makes you happy,' or, 'Whatever you want, sweetheart.'

The Amiables, falling into the Receptive/Agreeable quadrant, are the 'nice guys' of the world. Amiables do not want to disappoint anyone, so when you are negotiating with them, they can send you the wrong signals about a deal. As a result of their inclination to be kind, they do not like to say 'no'. This makes it difficult to gauge how they really feel about your proposal.

Negotiators continually fall into the trap of thinking that by not saying 'no', an Amiable means 'yes'. You need to ensure that you understand everyone's issues and concerns. Once you can show that your proposal addresses their issues, they will be happy to give you a clear 'yes' answer – they like others to have what they want. As with the Expressives, who are also 'warm' people, you need to tie the deal down as quickly as possible.

The opposite style to an Amiable is a Driver. An Amiable may aggravate the Driver, while a Driver is almost sure to wound the Amiable.

If you are an Amiable, in business people will love you but leave you, because they perceive you as not being able to make decisions. A bit more directness, albeit in your own kind manner, will serve you well.

### Drivers (Quadrant 3)
*The Greedy Bitch and the Game Player*
Drivers as birds would be hawks, and as animals, great white sharks.

Drivers are direct, independent, organised, determined, focused, pragmatic, loyal, results-orientated, demanding, critical, pushy, harsh, aggressive and competitive, among their many other characteristics.

Their favourite saying is: 'Don't make your problem my problem.' (Or even, 'You are confusing me with someone who cares.')

If you are negotiating with someone who is Aggressive and Sceptical, you will be dealing with a Driver. They will be cynical about what you are saying and, because they are forceful by nature, conflict and confrontation are never far away. They are comfortable with this kind of discord, but if you are not a Driver, it could make you feel uneasy. They will drive a hard bargain, but you must not back down (if you do, they will bulldoze you), nor must you meet 'fire with fire' (all hell may well break loose).

You need to be fully prepared with the facts and figures. Drivers will want to be able to measure value for value, so be sure that you can show what they will get, and what you expect, in quantitative terms. At a personal level, try to behave unemotionally and assertively, which will help to keep the meeting constructive and reduce the tension. On the upside, Drivers are decisive. Of all the behavioural styles, the one who will give you a direct answer, and is most likely to honour their word, is the Driver.

The opposite style to a Driver is an Amiable, so be careful in pitting these two styles against each other in a negotiation. If they are on the same side, they bring balance to the team.

If your style is that of a Driver, pay attention to the pleasantries of the meeting and the feelings of the other people in the room, and guard against appearing arrogant. I am a Driver, so I need to be careful not to come across as a rude git.

### Analyticals (Quadrant 4)
*Info Junkie Jude and Can't Close Colleen*
Analyticals as birds are owls, and as animals they are badgers.

Analyticals, among other traits, are respectful, tactful, good listeners, obedient, persistent, industrious, logical, systematic, orderly, deliberate, organised, detailed, stubborn, cautious, tedious and somewhat anal.

Their favourite saying is: 'I need to think about that.' (Or even: 'If only I had more information.')

As Agreeable and Sceptical, Analyticals are cautious and will want a lot of detail and information from you. They need time to consider all the facets of your proposal, especially the value they will get in exchange for the value you expect. Include as many facts and figures as possible. Analyticals need to be sure that they are making a decision that is fair and well thought-through. This takes time, which you may not always have.

To get an Analytical to engage with you and give you a decision, you need to actively check if they need more information and, if they do, provide it. You should be gentle but firm if they are disappearing in a puff of Oozlum detail. Push softly for an answer, as pushing too hard will provoke their stubborn side. Quantify, if you can, how important it is for them to make a decision.

The opposite of an Analytical is an Expressive. Combining the two into a single negotiating team is very sound practice, provided that the individuals respect each other.

If you are Analytical, you need to feel personally comfortable with the people you deal with, but, like the Amiable, try to communicate your decisions more openly. And watch out for that stubborn streak.

As it's not possible to 'brand' people accurately, you will find that even if individuals belong to the same behavioural category, e.g. Amiables, there will be substantial differences between them. Using Amiables as an example, a person who is very Receptive, but only mildly Agreeable (i.e. they are on the Agreeable axis but tend towards the Aggressive side of Agreeable), can become quite 'expressive' when she is in a social environment.

When people relax or are under pressure, their behaviour changes – a Driver may become more Analytical, or an Expressive more like a Driver, and so on. This is what I referred to earlier as *un*general behaviour.

Despite my temptation to do so, I am going to avoid getting into the 'secondary' styles – that level of analysis requires another chapter at least – as we do have enough information with just the 'primary' four styles to negotiate more effectively.

For fun, though, let's take a look at the *eight different deal divas* you might come across in the real world.

## EIGHT DEAL DIVAS OF NOTE
### 1. The Director
It's all about 'Lights, Camera, Action, Cut!' with this diva. When she negotiates a deal, she wants you to be able to present your ideas in thirty seconds or less (what is called an 'elevator pitch') or on the back of a cigarette box. If your proposal doesn't excite her, you cease to exist in her life – and you don't get a second chance, until she forgets and you can start all over. If she's interested in your ideas, she will turn on the charm. She will woo you, tell you about all the great plans she has for the two of you, and make you lots and lots of promises. When it comes to signing the deal, though, she is going to want you to sell your grandma's soul to get anything near what she promised you. If you try to point this out to her, she will get quite vicious and accuse you of trying to change the deal, or of reneging on an agreement, or of being a dishonourable and untrustworthy negotiator. You either have to sign a bad deal or walk away. If you hadn't already guessed, the Director is a hard-core Expressive.

### 2. Ms Mind Changer
Also an Expressive, Ms Mind Changer will enthusiastically discuss lots of alternatives with you. When it comes to the negotiation, she will give you everything you want and make a few demands in return. Once you have an agreement, she'll say, 'Deal done. Now let's go and celebrate with a glass of champers or twenty.' Off you go, drink merrily and become best friends. When you call her the next day to confirm the deal, she says she's very excited about it but can't talk now and will call you later. She doesn't call. The next day you phone again. She's warm but still busy. She again promises to phone back, but doesn't. The next day she is a bit cool, and from the fourth or fifth day, she doesn't take your calls. What have you done wrong? Nothing. She probably got bored at some point and agreed to a deal that she now realises she doesn't like. Ms Mind Changer won't know how to tell you

that the deal is off or that it needs to be renegotiated without looking like an idiot, so she cuts you dead. Go somewhere else – or wait until she has forgotten about this deal and start again.

## 3. Mrs Santa Claus

Negotiating with Amiable Mrs Claus is a pleasure initially. She is very happy with the deal and delighted to give you everything you want. When you realise that the deal is one-sided and you try to give her something to balance the value-for-value equation, she says, 'Don't be silly, sweetie. I don't expect anything from you.' Something niggles you about the deal, but you're not sure what or why. Could it be that, because she gave you what you wanted so easily, you wonder whether you asked for enough? Is your price perhaps too cheap? Before you sign the deal, you decide to test the water and, sure enough, she gives you more. You push the envelope, and she smiles and hands over. You are now feeling seriously unsettled, but you recognise you've got a dream deal and that you had best get it signed off. You present Mrs Claus with the paperwork, and that's when she tells you she just has to pop upstairs and have it rubber-stamped. In your heart you know that there is no way any stamp-holder will approve the deal. Have you blown your chances completely with your greedy deal?

## 4. Helpful Hilda

You like Helpful Hilda as soon as you meet her. She is a lovely, warm person who is incredibly obliging with information. She answers all your questions, shares anecdotes about everyone involved in the decision, and even tells you what you should and should not include in your proposals. She is always pleased to see you and invariably offers you a cup of tea and a chat when you visit. Helpful Hilda is a pleasure to do business with and you build a good relationship while you negotiate the deal. When everything is more or less agreed, she suggests you come back in a week's time to finalise the agreement. While waiting in reception to sign the deal – or so you think – you bump into an ex-colleague who now works for a competitor. Your former colleague tells you that she is dealing with a lovely woman who has been ever so kind in helping her to close a deal. You then realise that you have both been talking to the same person about the same deal. Helpful Hilda has generously been guiding two (or more?) people. How does she unravel the mess when you raise this with her? She postpones the deal. Going directly to Hilda's boss is going to cause problems in your relationship, but do you have a choice?

**5. The Greedy Bitch**
As you walk into her office, you realise that this is going to be a tough negotiation. The Greedy Bitch does not waste time with any niceties, such as saying hello or asking you how you are – she dives straight into the deal. She starts by making a demand without offering you anything in return. You figure that if you give her that one item, she'll appreciate your act of generosity and be more reasonable. And guess what? The Greedy Bitch just demands another concession, and then another and another. Eventually you point out to her that the deal favours her disproportionately and that it is not one your boss will accept. She has the cheek to say to you, 'Well then, why did you agree to the concessions?' She starts ranting and raving about people who come into her office with no authority to sign off on deals and says to you that in future she wants to meet with your boss. To placate her, you take the deal away to have it signed off by your boss – and that is when the trouble really starts. But, as she told you, she couldn't care less. Think she's a Driver by any chance?

**6. The Game Player**
You have worked extremely hard to close this deal and you now get to meet with the person who will give you the final decision. After having been mauled before by the Greedy Bitches, you've made sure that this deal represents value for both sides. You hope that the Game Player is going to sign the agreement as it stands. It is your financial year-end in a week's time and you really need the deal to be finalised. The Game Player looks you in the eyes and says, 'If you want me to sign this deal within the week, I want a further 20 per cent discount.' Twenty per cent takes all your profit out of the deal – and you are affronted by what you consider

to be blackmail. You try to persuade her that if you give any further discount, you will make almost nothing on the deal. All she says is, 'Don't make your problem my problem.' She appears completely emotionless, and you sense that she will play this game of cat and mouse (with you being Minnie) for as long as it takes for her to get what she wants. Do you walk away from the deal or roll over? In the real-life situation on which this story is based, the salesperson 'surrendered'. Oops.

### 7. Info Junkie Jude

You know that Info Junkie Jude is an Analytical, so you have been careful to include as much information as you can in your proposals and during the negotiation. She has crunched and munched each piece and then asked for more data on this and more background on that. Then she comes up with something completely different. When you ask her why, she says that she's not certain the original brief was correct and she needs more alternatives. Back to the drawing board you go to research what it is that she wants now. You proudly present her with the new information, and she examines the original brief again. And again. And so it continues until you limp to a very detailed, very long agreement. And once more she hums and haws and says she's not clear on this and that, and just when you are about to kill either her or yourself, she tells you that she is satisfied with the deal.

### 8. Can't Close Colleen

Negotiating with Can't Close Colleen is a mixed blessing. She is prepared to meet with you and discuss – for hours – the ins and outs of your proposal. She carefully analyses all the data and examines the facts, and then is willing to give you what you want – without too much of a haggle or a fight. You think the deal is done. Not so. Two days later you get a call from her, saying that she has thought some more about the deal and needs to clarify a few things that you discussed. You thought you had agreed, not 'discussed'. You meet again to talk through her concerns, and finally she says she is happy. A couple of days later you get an email querying some small point in the document. And on and on it goes. You're not sure if she is unhappy with the deal, or if she is delaying the decision for some other reason. You decide to call her up and ask her what is troubling her. She says that she just wants to make certain there is value for both parties in the deal. After another lengthy discussion, you are now sure she is satisfied. And then you get another email. It's time to either pull out your hair or go over her head.

## YOUR BEHAVIOURAL STYLE AND YOUR NEGOTIATING STYLE

We have had a bit of fun with the extremes of the four behavioural styles, but it's time to get serious. You should by now be able to identify your personal style – are you an Expressive, an Amiable, a Driver or an Analytical? If you are battling to decide between two styles, choose the one that *best* describes you in business or serious mode. If you are adamant that there is an equal amount of every style in you, I've got bad news, babe: the only person you will find smack-bang in the middle of the four quadrants is your classic psychopath. Yes, we do all have a bit of each style, but you will have a primary style and a secondary style, and we are concentrating on primary styles. If you *really* can't figure out your style, ask anyone (except a complete stranger) if you are generally:

- Aggressive (i.e. A-Type, competitive, tense, dominant); or
- Agreeable (i.e. B-Type, cooperative, easy-going, passive).

Now ask them if you are generally:
- Receptive (i.e. extroverted, impulsive, warm, spontaneous); or
- Sceptical (i.e. introverted, considered, self-controlled, cool).

Take the two words they have chosen for you and plot them on the diagram on page 123 that shows the four quadrants and the name of each style. If you don't agree with their analysis, this is because, even though you know they are right, you want to be another style. Go with the style they have selected for you for now. If you are still in doubt, you are an Analytical. Trust me.

Below are the areas you need to focus on for *your* negotiating style. All you really need to do is to *maximise* your strengths – make them even stronger – and be aware of your areas of weakness. Awareness is enough to kick-start the unconscious mind into changing what you need or want to change. For your interest, I have also included how the different styles tend to value themselves at an individual level.

| EXPRESSIVE: YOUR NEGOTIATING AREAS OF ATTENTION ||
| --- | --- |
| PLUS | MINUS |
| **1. Persuasive; verbal**<br>Your convincing way with words means that you can easily persuade people to give you what you want. Always try to use your fabulous powers of persuasion before you negotiate. | **1. Dramatic; overreactive**<br>Not everything is a big drama or catastrophe. Try to temper being theatrical with being inspiring. Negotiation is conflict-ridden enough without you adding to the chaos. |
| **2. Influential; confident**<br>People believe what you say, so if you ensure that you are consistent when negotiating, you will close quicker and better deals. Inconsistency breeds mistrust and compromises your ability to influence. | **2. Undisciplined; vague**<br>Although you come up with great ideas, your low boredom threshold means you don't follow your ideas through to the detail level. Resist the temptation to change tack halfway through. Use a methodology that helps you stick to your plan when you negotiate. |
| **3. Creative**<br>Your ability to generate ideas helps you create all the variables you could ever need to use in negotiations. Prepare the variables in advance and you will be brilliant. | |
| **How you value yourself**<br>Expressives are great self-promoters and find it easy to establish their credibility. Be careful not to oversell yourself relative to what you can deliver. ||

| AMIABLE: YOUR NEGOTIATING AREAS OF ATTENTION ||
| PLUS | MINUS |
|---|---|
| **1. Patient**<br>Your good-natured patience serves you well in negotiations. Use this to out-wait the other party. They may well lose interest and give you what you want in order to close the deal. | **1. Indecisive**<br>Negotiation is usually linked to conflict. Indecision will exacerbate any conflict. If you want to restore the concord, you need to make a decision on a deal more quickly. |
| **2. Flexible**<br>Negotiations deadlock or fail because people become intransigent and dig in on a position. Your ability to find alternative options (*not* common ground) can be used to great effect in a negotiation. Trust your intuition on where and when flexibility is required. | **2. Avoid confrontation**<br>Confrontation is counter to your character, but avoiding it (or delaying dealing with it) can escalate tensions. Combine your desire for equilibrium with the facts and details to help you face confrontation confidently. A decision, even sometimes the wrong one, will ease tensions. |
| **3. Supportive; cooperative**<br>You really do care that everyone gets value from a deal. Use your warm nature to encourage the other party to tell you their issues when negotiating. If you know what these are, you can get everything you want by giving the other party what they want. | |

**How you value yourself**
You tend to hope that others will recognise your value and reward you appropriately. You are modest and self-effacing, and while these are admirable qualities, you need to sell yourself more than you do. Have faith in your abilities.

# DEAL *Diva*

| DRIVER: YOUR NEGOTIATING AREAS OF ATTENTION ||
|---|---|
| **PLUS** | **MINUS** |
| **1. Organised; plan well** <br> The key to a successful negotiation is a structure or process. Use your planning ability to control the negotiation and to drive it to the conclusion that you want. Recognise the deal when it is done, and stop pushing for more. | **1. Dominant; aggressive** <br> Your antagonistic style can be extremely threatening to others. If they are anxious, they will clam up and not tell you their issues. This usually means that you throw all sorts of concessions at them to get them to agree to what you want, which can get very expensive. |
| **2. Direct; candid** <br> The best way to get what you want in a negotiation is to tell the other party. You are no shrinking violet here, but remember to include an incentive for them if need be. Your straight-talking style also encourages the other side not to challenge you on your word. | **2. Insensitive; tactless** <br> Negotiation is not just about hard facts and figures. The human element is just as important. If you ignore the soft issues, you can damage relationships irreparably, to the point that nobody wants to do further deals with you. |
| **3. Determined; focused** <br> Persistence and focus are crucial in negotiation. Your capacity for perseverance will reward you with deals that others may have forsaken. Just remember to stop when you've got what you want. | |

**How you value yourself**
Using your sheer force of character is not always the best way to demonstrate your value. Being more gracious and less intense will help you to showcase your talents more effectively.

## ANALYTICAL: YOUR NEGOTIATING AREAS OF ATTENTION

| PLUS | MINUS |
|---|---|
| **1. Precise; systematic**<br>Your persistent and detailed approach helps to ensure that all issues are covered during a negotiation. Allow for creativity and flexibility in the process and you will hold the negotiation in your hands. | **1. Anal; over-cautious**<br>'Analytical' doesn't contain the word 'anal' for no reason. In striving for detail and perfection you can become the Oozlum bird. Negotiation is driven by intuition as much as by process. Avoid doing everything 'by the book'. |
| **2. Diplomatic; good listener**<br>With your tactful and attentive style, you are able to build relationships with other parties quite easily. Be sure to incorporate the information you gather from this into the negotiation. Offering them what they want helps you to get what *you* want. | **2. Stubborn; unresponsive**<br>When someone annoys you, you tend to dig in your heels and become impassive. Negotiation is a dialogue and, in order to be successful, requires your flexibility and participation. Stonewalling inevitably leads to deadlock, and this does not help you to get what you want – unless you want the status quo to remain, of course. |
| **3. Deliberate; industrious**<br>The combination of hard work and deliberation serves you well. Getting to a negotiated deal can be a real slog and, in many instances, it is only due to your conscientious diligence that a result will be achieved. | |

**How you value yourself**
Your reluctance to promote yourself does not serve you. If you do not tell someone what you are capable of, how are they supposed to know? People are not always as observant as you would hope.

## BE TRUE TO WHO YOU ARE

Take the time to understand how you typically behave in the workplace, socially and at home, and think about how you *want* to behave. If there is cognitive dissonance (i.e. there is a disconnect), you can fix it. Don't be unkind to yourself, though – a few gentle reminders will do the trick. 'I will not drink too much champagne and behave outrageously. I will not drink too much champagne and behave outrageously. I will not drink too much champagne and behave outrageously.' That sort of thing.

Adjusting your behaviour to accommodate someone else's behavioural style does not mean you are selling out. If you want to play smart – and you wouldn't be reading this book if you didn't – shift *your* behaviour to make sure that you get the deal you want. Talking to people in their own behavioural language gives you power, and power is a very important factor in negotiating. You know that it is impossible to change someone else – only they have control over whether they change or not. Focus on that which you *can* control – *your* attitude, *your* perceptions and *your* behaviour – to get what you want, when you want it and how you want it.

Be prepared to use a little stereotyping to help you analyse your behaviour and that of other people. Categorisation is how we order our world. It's not like a bit of pigeonholing is going to end mankind as we know it. Be aware of the impact your behaviour has on those around you – there is positive and negative in every style – and be prepared to modify your behaviour to make the most of the diva you are.

Remember at all times that we are who we are, and who we are is simply and absolutely perfect. Okay, sometimes our behaviour leaves a lot to be desired, but that does not make our essence – our soul – bad or flawed. Not for one minute do I advocate changing your character. Always be true to yourself, but if you modify the *behaviour* that does not benefit you, you will be able to experience the most satisfying and serene existence possible.

Oh, and you will be able to maximise the deals you want too.

## Chapter 7

# HOW TO DEFINE THE DEAL YOU WANT

>'Be careful what you wish for. You might just get it.'
>– *Traditional proverb*

And now, ladies and divas, we have arrived at the first of the two chapters on 'how' – how to structure your negotiation, how to decide where you open and when you walk away, how to use carrots to best effect and how to organise your negotiating team. The plan, you will be pleased to hear, is to keep the 'how' sections as simple and easy as possible.

Here is an open secret – *to get what you want, you must know* what *you want*.

If you have read books on the laws of attraction, manifestation or affirmations, you will know that you need to be specific about what it is that you want. Negotiation is no different. To be successful, not only must you have a clear idea of what it is that you want, you must also be prepared to be flexible. Samuel Langhorne Clemens, aka Mark Twain (*American satirist and writer; 1835–1910*), said in *A Connecticut Yankee in King Arthur's Court* in 1889 that 'She was wise, subtle, and knew more than one way to skin a cat.' As a bunny hugger and veg-head, I find this old saying a little offensive, but it is good advice – to get what you want, you must know many ways to obtain cat skin, so to speak.

There is a lovely scene in the movie *P.S. I Love You* when Daniel, the Harry

Connick Jr character, asks Holly, played by Hilary Swank, what it is that women really want. Holly whispers to Daniel that women have no idea. Daniel triumphantly punches the air and says, 'I knew it!' Women *are* often accused of not knowing what they want, but, according to Mimi Pond (*American writer and cartoonist*), 'What women want are shoes.' Hallelujah, sister, but in addition to shoes, I believe women have a pretty good idea as to what they want – they just don't always know how to ask for it.

I have spent a lot of time coaching you to say, '*If you* do *this* for me, *then I* will do *that* for you.' *That* is how you ask for what you want! But the 'this' and the 'that' in the 'If you …' statement must be clearly defined. Think back to the purple and pink carrots – silly example, I know, but did you notice how specific I was being about *what* and *how many*?

Women are reluctant to use 'If you … then I …' because they don't want to come across as pushy or greedy. Women fear to tread where their male counterparts just rush in. We need to be prepared to be the fool too – we must be far braver about asking for what we want. If the reason you don't ask is because you believe you are not worthy, go back to the beginning of the book and start again. Women are worthy. Women add value. Without women, the human race would cease to exist (we can always replace men with sperm banks). We are friggin' goddesses!

Okay, ladies, it's time to go and get what you want.

## HAVE A STRATEGY FOR *HOW* TO GET WHAT YOU WANT

When companies define how they are going to achieve the results they want, they plan a 'go to market' strategy. You, too, need to have a strategy that outlines *how* you intend to get what you want. Strategy is an incredibly complex subject and I promised to keep things simple, so if you are a strategist reading this book, please forgive me for the minimalism.

Imagine that you want to buy a new house. The critical factors you will consider will typically be price, area and size. You will then set about looking for the house, and the negotiation will follow.

In the case of companies, their sales and negotiation strategy will be depicted in a model that looks something like this:

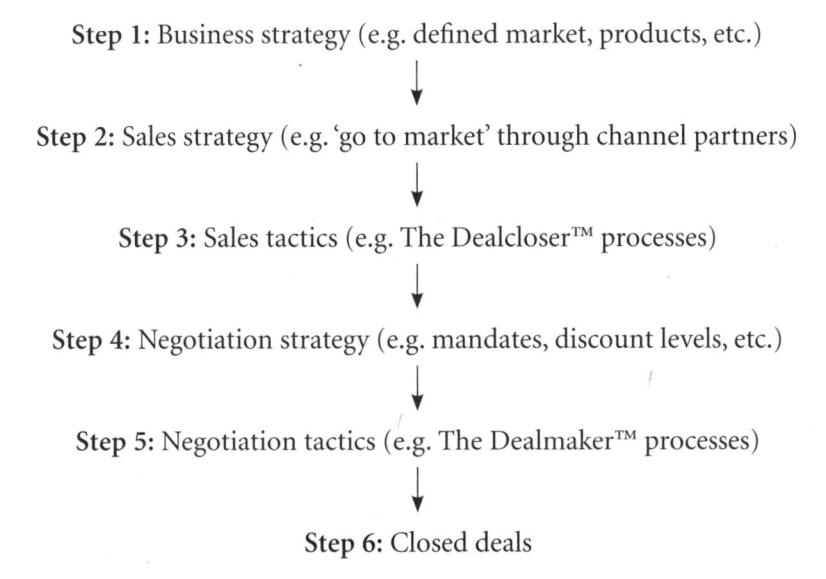

**Step 1:** Business strategy (e.g. defined market, products, etc.)
↓
**Step 2:** Sales strategy (e.g. 'go to market' through channel partners)
↓
**Step 3:** Sales tactics (e.g. The Dealcloser™ processes)
↓
**Step 4:** Negotiation strategy (e.g. mandates, discount levels, etc.)
↓
**Step 5:** Negotiation tactics (e.g. The Dealmaker™ processes)
↓
**Step 6:** Closed deals

If you had to draw a diagram for the strategic steps to your new house, it would be much like the one above. Surprisingly, individual strategies can be quite similar to those used in business. Your big picture ('business strategy') would define the price, location and size of the property.

In basic terms, your 'sales strategy and tactics' could be along the following lines: As you are in no hurry to buy, you will take a long-term view of the market, watch which houses don't seem to be selling, wait for the seller to have (assumed) time constraints, and then go in with a cheeky offer.

Your 'negotiation strategy' may be to start as low as possible, without putting yourself too far out of the ball park, and then move up if you have no choice. Your negotiating tactics would be that every time you have to increase an offer, you will ask for something to improve your deal – such as the seller leaving all his tennis racquets and balls behind for the tennis court, or including the outdoor furniture, or paying the water and lights for an extra month.

Your 'closed deal' should, ideally, end up with you owning a great house at a very good price – your reward for planning properly!

## USE A PROCESS TO DEFINE *WHAT* DEAL YOU WANT

Now that you have a rough handle on the strategy, you need to use a process to define *what* deal you are going to negotiate. In detail.

It is essential – and I mean *critical* – to determine your strategy and define the process for the deal *before* you start negotiating with the other side. If you go into a negotiation without a clear idea of *what* (defined deal) you want and *how* (strategy) you are going to get it, you are going to get your backside kicked. I am quite happy to show you the footprints on my ass from when I have not planned properly.

For the purpose of showing you 'how' to do this, I suggest we stick with one example – how to negotiate the purchase of a house. I thought about using a salary negotiation, but, dear diva, you've already got that one licked!

There are three steps in the process you need to use to define your negotiation. Nothing could be simpler:

**Step 1:** The Issues
**Step 2:** The Ball Park
**Step 3:** The Players

Note the change to the use of capital letters with some of the words. From now on, for the important stuff, caps will apply!

## STEP 1: THE ISSUES

In the section on 'the power of carrots', I said that when we got to the 'how' of negotiating, particularly defining the Ball Park, you would learn that there are two types of carrots, or incentives: Key Issues (the big carrots) and Secondary Issues (the Marbles – or small carrots or carrot slices). We have arrived at that point!

The *first task* in step 1 is to identify *all* the issues that would be important in this specific deal – and I mean *all* of them. Please keep in mind that there will be factors other than money or price that you also need to consider.

In the 'buying a house' case, we have already got the first five of our issues from the strategy notes above. I have added all the other issues I could think up. As you can see, I have 'dumped' them below (i.e. they are not in any specific order – just jotted down as they occurred to me). If you were doing this list, I would recommend that you follow the same process.

1. Location.
2. Price.
3. Size of garden.
4. Size of house.
5. Cluster complex vs stand-alone house.
6. Security.
7. Style of house.
8. Condition of house.
9. New or renovation potential or (as my man says) bulldozer potential.
10. Good staff quarters.
11. Lots of garaging.
12. Storage space.
13. Walling.
14. Quiet or noisy area.
15. Any info on neighbours.
16. No schools nearby.
17. Does my existing furniture fit?
18. Pool or Jacuzzi.
19. Tennis court.
20. High or low maintenance.
21. Proximity to busy roads.
22. Accessibility.
23. Occupation date.
24. Occupational rent.
25. Proximity to shops.
26. North or south facing.

**27.** Privacy or view.
**28.** Quality of kitchen (for my man).
**29.** Entertainment area (for me).
**30.** Snob appeal (for me again).
**31.** Work-from-home space.
**32.** Single floor or stairs.
**33.** Number of bathrooms and bedrooms.

The *second task* in step 1 is to rank and prioritise the list. The trick here is to pick out the *Key Issues* – those that are of the greatest importance to you. Depending on the negotiation, the number of Key Issues will range from one or two to about five or six.

The Key Issues are usually the ones you thought of first – those that are front of mind. You will know when you have identified the Key Issues, because there will be a big gap between the last Key Issue you think of and the next most important one. The issues that are left are called the *Secondary Issues*. Put the Secondary Issues aside for the moment, and let's go back to the Key Issues.

Below are what my Key Issues would be if I were looking for a house. Bear in mind, though, that my ideal house is around 500 $m^2$ on half an acre with one huge bedroom, a fabulous bathroom and a massive study, and the rest consisting of a kitchen and entertainment space. (In the lists that follow, I use the numbering from the list above to illustrate the prioritisation process.)

**1.** Location.
**2.** Price.
**3.** Size of garden.
**4.** Size of house.
**5.** Cluster complex vs stand-alone house.
**6.** Security.
**14.** Quiet or noisy area.
**27.** Privacy or view.

# HOW TO DEFINE THE DEAL YOU WANT

As you can see, I have eight items. This is probably too many, so I need to prioritise again. Your issues might differ completely from mine (my hubby would definitely have 'kitchen' on his list), but my top five would be:

1. Location.
2. Price.
4. Size of house.
3. Size of garden.
5. Cluster complex vs stand-alone house.

Once you have identified your Key Issues (still keeping the Secondary Issues apart for the moment), you are now ready to enter the Ball Park.

## STEP 2: THE BALL PARK

Before you rush out and start buying your new house, there is another level of planning that needs to take place. Above I referred to a 'Ball Park'. We all seem to know what a Ball Park is, but how do you define it in negotiating terms?

In our example, the Ball Park for the 'price' priority would be the highest price you are prepared to pay for the house versus the lowest offer the seller will accept. This defines the boundaries within which the deal will be struck.

If you had a crystal ball and could 'see' the seller's lowest price, this is the point where you would expect to do the deal. If the seller, on the other hand, knew your highest price, that is where he would want the deal to be closed.

In the real world, we generally do not know the other person's limits, so we can determine only our own Ball Park. We should try to 'best-guess' the other party's Ball Park. I know it's not very scientific, but dealmaking is a large part art and only a small part science.

Determining the Ball Park takes time. You need to conduct research and give the matter considerable thought. In our example, you will need to know at what prices similar houses in the area have been sold, understand the market trends (for example, are house prices dropping because of the economy?) and the like. You also need to decide on the maximum you will pay for the house, the boundaries of the location you will consider, and the biggest versus smallest sizes for the house and the garden.

## Ball Park – Key Issues

The next task in defining the Ball Park is to prepare the following positions for *each* Key Issue:

1. **Likely:** this is your target, or what you realistically expect to get (or pay, in the case of the house). Always start preparing your Ball Park using your 'Likely' position.
2. **Bottom Line:** prepare this second. It is your walk-away position – the point beyond which you will not go (your limit or minimum/maximum).
3. **Opening:** do this one last. It is the best possible outcome you could want (i.e. the lowest price you would pay for a house). If you were negotiating your salary, it would be the highest salary imaginable. You would still need to be realistic, or you could find yourself 'outside of the Ball Park'.

The easiest way in which to draw up your Ball Park is in a table format. Here is a fictitious example, assuming I was looking for a fancy house in Johannesburg, and applying my earlier priorities.

| ISSUE | # (priority) | OPENING (do this last) | LIKELY (do this first) | BOTTOM (do this second) |
|---|---|---|---|---|
| Location | 1 | Inanda | Illovo/Inanda | Illovo/Inanda/Atholl |
| Price | 2 | R4 million | R5.5 million | R7.5 million |
| Size of house | 3 | 500 m$^2$ | 450 m$^2$ | 400 m$^2$ |
| Size of garden | 4 | Half-acre | Half-acre | Half-acre |
| Stand-alone house | 5 | Yes | Yes | Yes |

What do you notice about the table? Check your observations against the points below:

1. **There must be a reason behind the Opening and Bottom Line values.** You need to be able to substantiate your Opening and walk-away positions. In my example, I don't have a price of R3 million as my 'Opening', because as much as I would like to pay that little, it would be outside the Ball Park for the area and thus a waste of everyone's time. I also won't spend more than R7.5 million, because that is all the money I have, including my mortgage and the loan from the dog.
2. **The range of 'location' is quite small.** Position is my number-one priority. I will keep looking until I find a house in these areas. If there is a fabulous house for sale in the next suburb, I will not even go and look at it.
3. **I have reprioritised my Key Issues.** On reflection, size of house has become more important than garden size.
4. **I am not flexible on the size of the garden.** I do not want a property that is unmanageably big, but I need a minimum of half an acre for my two bull terrorists.
5. **I am not flexible on a stand-alone house.** I do not want a complex, an apartment or a farm. I want a stand-alone house.
6. **The chance of me achieving all my Opening issues is unlikely.** Only in my dreams would I find a house in Inanda the size that I want for R4 million!
7. **If I had to settle for all my Bottom Line items, I would be getting a lousy deal.** If I paid R7.5 million for a small house in Atholl, I would not be happy with the deal *as a whole*.
8. **The deal I am most likely to get will be a mix of my Opening, Likely and Bottom Line positions.** If I can find a house in Atholl for R4 million that is the size I want, I would be a happy camper.

Even when you are armed with a broad strategy and a Ball Park for your Key Issues, you are not yet ready to start negotiating. What about the list of all the other issues, which we put aside earlier?

### Ball Park – Secondary Issues

For the sake of clarity, the 'issues' you have in a negotiation can equate to incentives (or disincentives) or carrots. The Key Issues are the big and important carrots, and the Secondary Issues are the carrot slices, Marbles, variables or small issues. The Key Issues are the 'must haves', and the Secondary Issues are the 'nice to haves'. Deals should always be won or lost only over the Key Issues. The Secondary Issues should not be deal-breakers. Got it? Good.

So, what do we do with the Secondary Issues? How do we 'play' with our Marbles? Like a child, dearest, like a child.

The *next step* in defining the Ball Park is to draw up another table, one that looks like this:

| MARBLES FOR ME TO GET | MARBLES FOR ME TO GIVE |
|---|---|
| | |

You now take all the carrots that are left on the 'buying a house' list (the other twenty-eight of the original thirty-three) and, using these twenty-eight items as prompts, prepare a list of Marbles (or small carrots) you can *get* from the other party, as well as a list of Marbles you can *give*, should you need to.

This is how it works. Let's take 'security' (priority no. 6 on the original list) as the example. It's no good putting 'gated community' on my 'Marbles-to-get' list. How the hell is the seller supposed to turn Katherine Street, a major road, into a boomed-off area? See what I put below. Get it? Here's another one – 'style of house'. Again, the seller can't convert concrete chic into Cape Dutch, but the 'style of house' can trigger some good ideas for my give/get Marbles lists.

I have only done a few samples for you. Try to do the rest yourself for practice. From here on, it becomes *your* example. Be as outrageously creative as you can – get in touch with your inner child!

| SECONDARY ISSUES | MARBLES TO GET | MARBLES TO GIVE |
|---|---|---|
| • Security | Leave alarm system, or install outdoor passives, or pay alarm radio for one month | Take alarm system with them, or give them my old alarm |
| • Style of house | Paint house colour I want, or install wood front door | Can take fitted carpets or light fittings |
| • Occupation date | Within three months | Within three months |
| • Occupational rent | None | R20 000 or R40 000 per month after month two, or % of purchase price |
| • Condition of house | Have carpets steamed, or strip down to original floors | Remove the rubbish previous owners leave behind |
| • New, renovate, dozer | Pay for bulldozing | Can take cactii with them |
| • Good staff quarters | | |
| • Lots of garaging | | |
| • Storage space | | |
| • Walling | | |
| • Quiet or noisy area | | |
| • Info on neighbours | | |
| • No schools nearby | | |
| • Fit of existing furniture | | |

| SECONDARY ISSUES | MARBLES TO GET | MARBLES TO GIVE |
|---|---|---|
| • Pool or Jacuzzi | | |
| • Tennis court | | |
| • High/low maintenance | | |
| • Proximity to roads | | |
| • Accessibility | | |
| • Proximity to shops | | |
| • North or south facing | | |
| • Privacy or view | | |
| • Quality of kitchen | | |
| • Entertainment area | | |
| • Snob appeal | | |
| • Work-from-home space | | |
| • Single floor or stairs | | |
| • No. bedrooms/baths | | |

Have you got an idea brewing in the back of your brain on how to use these Marbles? Can you recall the purple/pink carrots dialogue? Here is the same principle with the house example.

    A seller is asking R4.9 million for a near-perfect house in Atholl. The house has been on the market for a while and the economy has experienced a downturn. You decide to offer the seller R3.8 million for these reasons. You are also deducting a bit because the house is not in Illovo or Inanda (if it was, you would offer your R4-million Opening amount). The estate agent takes your offer to the seller and comes back to say that he wants R4.2 million (this is called a counter-offer). You increase your offer to R3.9 million *providing he paints the entire house.* He says that if you want the house painted, you must give him R4.1 million. You counter-offer with R4 million *and* a painted house *and* no occupational rent for the first two months. And the house is yours!

An important aside: You can always increase an offer on a house, but you can almost never make it less!

The power in getting what you want in a negotiation is to give the other side the Marbles and the value that *they* want, not the ones you would like to surrender. See if you can find out what they would like to have included on the Marbles list.

Always try to trade your Key Issues with their Key Issues, and use the Secondary Marbles to even out the deal – this is the essence of value-for-value dealmaking. Marbles are your negotiating leverage – they allow you to massage the deal into one with which you are fully satisfied.

For practice, go back to the salary-package example and figure out how you could repeat the exercise we have just done using the benefits as your Marbles. If you can't be bothered to do the exercise, don't be disappointed if you get less than you want in your next important deal – and the one after that, and after that. You really do need to practise creating your Key and Secondary Issues lists. Alternatively, of course, you could attend a course like The Dealdiva™ and be coached on how to do it.

You are nearly there, dear diva; you are *nearly* ready to go and kick ass in a negotiation. Just one more step before we get down and dirty in the actual face-to-face encounter.

## STEP 3: THE PLAYERS

There are plenty of pros and cons in either being part of a team or doing deals on your own. You need to weigh up which option will give you the most power and best advantages.

A rule of thumb is to take a person you trust along with you to keep track of the deal – that is, to make notes, watch for signs of flexibility, figure out the other party's agenda, and so on. But be careful – you don't want to take someone to a deal who gets too involved in the proceedings and loses all your hard-won ground!

If you are negotiating against a team, you may want to go in on your own and play divide and conquer with the other side. Equally, you may want a team of your own to give you support or to equalise the numbers. The team that you use (or don't use, as the case may be) can and will influence your power position.

Choosing the *right* team – or Players, as I prefer to call them – has a dramatic impact on your power. Players can positively affect the authority and legitimacy of your team, and they can also bring credibility to the team. They can, of course, also damage your position, so choose your Players wisely.

When you go in with a team, be sure to select one that is appropriate to the negotiation. If you are negotiating with the chief executive of a large organisation, you should think about taking along someone from your organisation who is on a similar level. But, be warned: top dogs want to be in charge, so even if they promise to sit quietly in the back and behave, in no time at all they will be running (or is that ruining?) the show.

Similarly, if the meeting is being attended by the monkeys and not the organ-grinders, you may want to hold your big guns back to use at a more apposite time. If the other side brings in experts, like lawyers, engineers or accountants, you should consider doing the same. Having to adjourn the whole time because you (or they) need technical advice can be very disruptive.

Regardless of whether or not you are flying solo or playing in a team, there are certain tasks that need to be performed in the negotiation. If you are on your own, these roles don't disappear – you need to make sure that *you* execute them. If you are in a team, you can allocate the tasks to your Players.

Imagine that you were part of the South African team that won the Rugby World Cup in 2007. The team consisted of people with distinct responsibilities. There were, among others, the captain (John Smit – yum #1), the vice-captain (Victor Matfield – yum #2), the coach (Jake White) and the South African Rugby board (management and selectors). Nobody (other than the selectors perhaps) tried to do the other person's job. We did not see Jake White running onto the field to get involved in a scrum. We did not see Victor Matfield take over as captain because he thought he could do a better job than John Smit. Okay, the selectors interfered constantly with Jake White, but, as I said, that is what bosses are wont to do.

There are roughly five sets of tasks in a negotiating team. As you read each one, think of the rugby team. A negotiating team is not exactly the same, but the association with a rugby team will help you to delineate the roles more easily. Here they are:

1. **Captain** – the dealmaker, leader or chief negotiator.
2. **Vice-captain** – the translator, summariser or controller.
3. **Coach** – the guide or observer.
4. **Manager** – the strategist or power base.
5. **Expert Advisors** – subject-matter authorities.

If you are working in a team, ideally you must have everyone involved in strategising and planning the deal.

## The Captain

The Captain is like a queen on a chessboard. She can really do anything she wants, but her primary function is to lead the team in the negotiating encounter. She will:
- Lead the discussions and negotiation.
- Persuade and trade.
- Make proposals and respond to proposals.
- Give information and engage in debate.
- Close the deal.

As the queen, though, she can pretty much perform whatever tasks she chooses, but the ones above are her specific responsibilities.

## The Vice-captain

The Vice-captain is the wingwoman, the second-in-command, the sidekick. She does about a third of the talking for her team. She has three distinct duties:

1. **Controls the process** – the stricter the protocols and processes of the negotiation, the less likely it will be to go off track. Also, a process helps to take the emotion and tension out of a situation. The agenda is one of the processes the Vice-captain controls.
2. **Asks the questions** – although the Captain decides whether to give information or not, the Vice-captain is tasked with *getting* the information the team needs. This means that she must be sure that questions have been prepared before the meeting, and that they get asked (by her, mostly).
3. **Recaps and summarises** – refer to the eight essential objectives of debate in the section entitled 'The Art of Communication' for the ideas around recapping and summarising. The number-one issue is to keep the summaries objective! Where the Captain gets to close the deal, the Vice-captain must finalise all the details *before* the close of the deal.

### The Coach

The Coach is literally tasked with guiding the team. To do so effectively, she must observe and not talk – in other words, she must behave like Jake White and resist the temptation to rush in and play the game. The problem is, the more she observes, the more she knows what is going on, and the more she has to resist getting directly involved.

The Coach listens carefully to the verbal communication, watches for clues and observes body language. Her task is to try to figure out the other party's issues. If the Coach can help her team to understand the other side's needs, her team will be in a position to offer the other side what they really want – which is often cheaper than guessing and then throwing carrots at them.

The Coach also usually takes the notes or minutes. When the team adjourns or calls for a time-out, the Coach finally starts speaking. Her express intent is to guide her colleagues and help them achieve the optimal value-for-value deal.

### The Manager

Where the Coach is the guide, the Manager is the power behind the throne. The Manager does not always attend the negotiations. As I said earlier, you need to decide whether to hold the big shots back for a more appropriate meeting or not. Although the Manager will not be involved in every negotiation, she is there behind the scenes. She ultimately decides strategy, hires and fires the team members, determines the mandate (in other words, the Ball Park – where you open and when you walk away), puts up the money and has the final authority.

## The Expert Advisors

These can be accountants, shareholders, lawyers, engineers, technicians, bankers, financiers, and so on. An Expert Advisor is someone who has specific expertise relative to the deal you are negotiating. You remember that advert for dry pasta where the mama is kept in the cupboard and only wheeled out to cook before being put back in the cupboard? That is how you need to use your Expert Advisors. Bring them in to do what they are skilled to do, then chase them out of the meeting. I have seen more negotiations wrecked by these Players than by anyone or anything else.

A property developer who attended one of our courses told me the story of a town planner he had brought in to meet with the Italian financier of a development project. Instead of advising on the regulations regarding the project, the town planner proceeded to tell the Italian about the corruption in the council, how ineffective the local authority was, and how much he despised the mayor. All these were his opinions, of course, but the net effect was that the Italian got on a plane, never to be seen again.

I experienced a similar situation when I was involved in negotiating the purchase of a German consulting company. The half-a-billion-rand deal had taken ages to bring to closure. At the end, as part of the finalisation before signing the contracts, both sides brought in their lawyers. The lawyer for the consulting company, who wanted us to refer to him as Herr Doctor Doctor (fat chance), wanted to show everyone how clever he was and proceeded to get into a battle of wits with our lawyer. Observing their lawyer pulling the deal apart, the sellers got scared and – after *two years* of negotiation – started questioning whether they should be doing the deal, whether we were trying to screw them, whether they weren't getting enough value, and, and, and …

I had chosen to be Coach (which I think is the most powerful position) and thus could see exactly what was happening. I pulled my boss, the Captain, aside and advised him to chase out both sets of lawyers. Once the lawyers were out of the room, we were able to put the deal back on track. Only when we had summarised the whole deal, from start to finish, did we let the lawyers back in – on condition that they gave only legal input.

**Home alone, or the whole tribe?**
If you are the single member of your 'team', you need to be Captain, Vice-captain, Coach, Manager and Expert Advisor. You can't leave out a role just because there is only you. If you ever get the opportunity to practise a role on its own, take it. This is the best way to get to grips with each function that gets performed in a negotiation.

If there are two of you, say you and a friend, or your partner, or a colleague, split the tasks between you – in a way that makes sense! You can't make the Coach, which is supposed to be a non-speaking role, the same person as the Captain (who does most of the talking). Double up the Captain as Manager and the Coach as the Vice-captain. Whoever is the subject-matter authority can be the Expert Advisor.

If there are twelve of you, you should have one Captain, one Vice-captain, one Manager, as many Expert Advisors as you need, and everyone else can be a Coach. I do think the Coaches are the most powerful people in the team as they are the ones who know what is *really* going on in a negotiation.

**The intelligent use of a team**
If you have the luxury of using a team, grab the opportunity with both hands, *but* choose your Players wisely. Your team members must understand the tasks they will be performing and must be disciplined enough to stick to them. There is nothing more unsettling for the Captain than having Coaches who talk, a Vice-captain who takes over, or a Manager who interferes or changes the mandate. A team is valuable only if each Player carries out the role she is meant to perform.

Try to find out as much as you can about the Players in the other team, and

# HOW TO DEFINE THE DEAL YOU WANT

then box clever. Look at the different behavioural styles of the opposite team and decide who, in your team, will perform what role. If the Captain of the other team is an Analytical, you know that he needs detail but is usually easy-going. If you want a cooperative meeting, do not make an Expressive your Captain. If you want to inject tension, choose Attila the Hen (a Driver) as Captain. If you want to build the relationship, pull Mother Teresa (an Amiable) out of the cupboard. Play the game in a way that gives you maximum power.

Even within your own team, there will be a natural dissonance between Amiables and Drivers, and Analyticals and Expressives. Consider the impact this will have on the planning (which is where you spend most of your time as a team) versus the face-to-face encounter.

A quick tip: Decide who will play what role early on in the deal cycle – before the preparation even begins, if possible. Being able to plan when you know that you will be the Captain or Coach changes the focus of your personal preparation.

If the decision on who will perform what role is *not* within your control, it doesn't mean that you can't show your colleagues and your boss what you are made of and suggest who should be allocated what role!

Now, dear diva, we are ready to meet with the other party and negotiate our little buns off.

## THE LAWYER AND THE DUCK

Now that we have in place our three-step process to define the negotiation – the Issues, the Ball Park and the Players – we are ready to learn about the 'Three-kick Rule'.

> A big-city lawyer went duck hunting in rural Tennessee. He shot and dropped a bird, but it fell into a farmer's field on the other side of a fence. As the lawyer climbed over the fence, an elderly farmer drove up on his tractor and asked him what he was doing.
>
> The litigator responded, 'I shot a duck and it fell in this field, and now I'm going to retrieve it.'

The old farmer replied, 'This is my property, and you are not coming over here.'

The indignant lawyer said, 'I am one of the best trial attorneys in the United States and, if you don't let me get that duck, I'll sue you and take everything you own.'

The old farmer smiled and said, 'Apparently you don't know how we settle disputes in Tennessee. We settle small disagreements with the "Three-kick Rule".'

'What is the "Three-kick Rule"?' the lawyer asked.

The farmer replied: 'Well, because the dispute occurs on my land, I get to go first. I kick you three times and then you kick me three times and so on back and forth until someone gives up.'

The attorney quickly thought about the proposed contest and decided that he could easily take the old codger. He agreed to abide by the local custom.

The old farmer slowly climbed down from the tractor and walked up to the attorney. His first kick planted the toe of his heavy steel work boot into the lawyer's groin and dropped him to his knees. His second kick to the midriff sent the lawyer's last meal gushing from his mouth. The lawyer was on all fours when the farmer's third kick to his rear-end sent him face first into a fresh cow pie.

The lawyer summoned every bit of his will and managed to get to his feet. Wiping his face with the arm of his jacket, he said, 'Okay, you old fart. Now it's my turn.'

The old farmer smiled and said, 'Nah, I give up. You can have the duck.'

Source unknown

## Chapter 8

## HOW TO NEGOTIATE FACE TO FACE

> 'I will tell you a secret: dealmaking beats working.
> Dealmaking is exciting and fun, and working is grubby.'
> – Dr Peter F. Drucker
> *(Austrian-born management theorist; 1909–2005)*

This is the part you've probably been waiting for – 'how' to conduct a face-to-face negotiation. It's the point at which you offer the other party the chance to give you what you want. If you read only the tips in this chapter, you will still be a much better negotiator. But I don't want you to be 'much better'; I want you to be a *deal diva*! A negotiating goddess!

As you may have realised, I like to refer to negotiating as a 'game'. We have talked about thinking (not behaving!) like a child, about playing with Marbles, and pretending we are a rugby team. Dr Peter Drucker is correct in what he says above, but negotiation and dealmaking only become fun when you are confident about what you are doing – when you understand the *planning*, the *engagement* and the *close*. If you know these three things, it doesn't matter what tricks and tactics the other party throws at you; you'll be able to play them with ease and confidence.

Now it's time to learn the rules of engagement – or what I call the negotiating 'encounter'.

## THE POWER OF THE PROPOSAL

In the section on 'power', I mentioned that there is inherent power in the trading process, and that trading is driven by proposals. To be a powerful dealmaker, you need to be able to make, and respond to, proposals. If proposals are so powerful, do you have any idea why I didn't include 'the power of the proposal' in the power section?

The answer is that, before you can plan effectively, you need to understand the power base. Only once you comprehend your power – and have ways to adjust that balance of power – can you start on your strategy and your Ball Park. And only *then* are you ready to play the ultimate power game: making proposals.

So now that you have your Ball Park, your 'give' and 'get' Marbles, and your team, you are ready to meet. Who goes first?

## WHO SHOULD MAKE THE FIRST MOVE?

To become an authority on a subject, you need to know as much as possible about your field. You need to read, research, study, practise, be coached and mentored, debate, postulate and much, much more. It is only when, like Michel Legrand (*French composer, conductor and pianist; 1932–*), you can say, 'The more I live, the more I learn; the more I learn, the less I know,' that you can give yourself a pat on the back for getting closer to being an expert.

It is my ambition to be a negotiating guru. Although I have been studying negotiation for over fifteen years, my learning is complicated by the 'experts', all of whom seem to have different views on who should make the first proposal. And although I do not consider myself a guru quite yet, this is an area about which I feel confident to talk with authority. *You* should go first. I learnt this, in part, as an instructor for Scotwork, but mostly at the school of hard knocks – in other words, from experience. My offer for you to see the scars on my backside still stands.

There are two exceptions to the 'you must make the first proposal' rule. The first is when you have no idea how much something is worth. Even then, I suggest you do your homework and try to find out. If you are genuinely not able to establish the value of something, wait to hear what the other person has to say first. Then postpone, do your homework and respond to their number.

The second exception is when you have screwed up. Let the other person tell you what they want you to do to put things right. Sometimes they will want an apology, and at other times it will be compensation. At least with compensation you have the opportunity to negotiate around giving them what they want. Customer research shows that it costs about six times as much to attract a new customer than it does to keep an existing one. Even if the unhappy party makes pretty outrageous demands, it might be cheaper to pay up than to find a new customer. Read the work of Dr Paul R. Timm if you're interested in more statistics on customer service.

Back to you making that first proposal. People in general, but women in particular, are reluctant to make the first move. Could it be because girls have been taught to wait for the marriage proposal? Perhaps, but I think it's more to do with these six reasons:

1. Women lack the confidence to ask for what they want – especially the Analyticals and Amiables.
2. Women don't always know what they want – they don't know how to plan properly.
3. Women can be doormats – the 'I am not worthy' brigade.
4. Women don't know how to value themselves.
5. Women are not sure how to make or receive proposals.
6. Women hope that, in waiting for the other person to go first, they will get a better deal.

We have addressed the first four of these points, and we are going to examine giving and receiving proposals in a moment, but, for now, we will focus on point 6.

DEAL *Diva*

## THE FIRST PROPOSAL

*Women hope that, in waiting for the other person to go first, they will get a better deal.* Women also hope that they will find Mr Darcy, win the Lotto and live happily ever after. Here is a true-life example.

I love auctions. I get swept up in the excitement and I invariably buy stuff I don't need, but I still love them. A good few years ago, my husband Simon wanted a new car. A gorgeous, almost-new Mercedes-Benz sports car was going on auction and Simon decided that if he could get it for a good price, he would buy it. I went along for the ride.

I also love cars. The faster and sleeker the better. Anyhow, on the day of the auction, Simon registers and gets his number. Lot number 1 comes up. It is a beautiful silver convertible BMW with all the trimmings. Despite the fact that I have a perfect blue BMW in the garage at home, I grab Simon's number, wave it in the air, and two minutes later I am the proud owner of a car I don't need. Simon is stressed. By the time the Mercedes comes up for sale, the thought of two new cars has Simon hyperventilating and he can't bring himself to bid. We go home, the wrong person with the new car.

Not being one to hang about, I do my homework and find out that if I sell my blue BMW privately, I can get in the region of, say (spot the clues!), R96 000. If I trade it in, I can get R84 000. So I have my Ball Park defined – best case: R96 000; worst case: R84 000.

As luck will have it, my long-term insurance broker, Gorgeous Greek George, calls on me a couple of days after my big purchase. Seeing the new convertible BMW *and* the old blue BMW, all George can say is, 'And now?' I tell him the story. George, who loves cars even more than I do, asks me how much I want for the blue car. *I make classic mistake number one.* Guess what I say? 'Make me an offer.' Why is this a mistake? Think about it. I know how much I want, but in asking George to 'make me an offer', I am hoping that he will offer me more than R96 000.

'Sixty-five thousand,' says George. I am seriously disappointed – and that's when *I make classic mistake number two.* I fib. I say that I have already had an offer of R90 000. George's reply? 'Well, I suggest you take it then.' And my conversation with George is over. I have lost a potential buyer. I made it too hard for George to save face after his cheeky offer of R65 000. If I had said upfront that the book value was R96 000, he might have negotiated with me – and the stress of finding the money for the new car would have disappeared. Who knows, but I did manage to sell it three weeks later for R92 000.

I said that I was hoping George would offer me more than R96 000. You probably think what happened serves me right for being greedy. But, whether you like to admit it or not, I bet you do the same thing. You go for a job interview and you don't tell the potential employer what you want; you wait for their offer *in the hope that it will be more than you expected*. We all do it – it's called human nature. Think about it, though – in asking George to make me an offer, in whose interests was he going to make the offer – his or mine? He also wanted a good deal, so of course he was going to make an offer that favoured him. Human nature.

Before you start feeling sorry for 'poor Simon' and wondering what happened to his new car, remember when I said that I would tell you about his unique decision-making style? Well, he decided that he didn't want a Mercedes after all; he wanted a Land Cruiser that he could use to go to the bush. In keeping with his character, Simon looked at Land Cruisers for *two years*. He even recruited his friend Mike Kelly to help him find a car. I reckon Simon and Mike eventually knew every second-hand Land Cruiser in Johannesburg by name. Finally a very clean Land Cruiser comes up for auction, and Simon goes to the sale (I join him, but only on condition that I will not touch his number nor try to buy anything). Simon dithers and dallies about the car – for no good reason, I might add – and heads home empty-handed.

Land Cruisers don't come up for auction all that often, so I was surprised. When I asked Simon why he didn't buy the car, he says he didn't feel like it, but he would get one the next time. The next time comes, off we go to the auction and guess what he buys? A brand-new, two-seater Porsche Carrera. Simon had never even mentioned the word 'Porsche' before. You try to figure it out.

Can you answer this question: Where in the Ball Park should you pitch your first proposal? For a clue, look back to the names I gave the columns that we drew up for the Ball Park. It is not called the 'Opening' position for nothing, ladies. Open as high as you can without getting thrown out of the Ball Park.

When you put your proposal on the table, the other party is going to want you to move, so starting at your 'Likely' position means that you can only slide down towards the 'Bottom Line'. Opening as high as possible gives you maximum flexibility, but remember that you need to keep the total package value in sight. Anytime anyone wants any movement from you, top the package up with your Marbles.

The 'nice guy' does not get the better deal; those who know their Ball Park and keep it creative and flexible get what they want.

## THE ART OF PROPOSITIONING

You have put your proposal on the table using the 'If you ... then I' format, and now it is time for the other party to respond. Will they accept your proposal as it stands? That would be fabulous, but they are more than likely going to expect you to move from your position. They will want you to give more or accept less, or maybe even change the composition of your proposal in some way.

How do you move from your Opening position without diminishing the value of your proposal or losing face? You take a few Marbles out of your pocket and give them what they want in exchange for what you want. You move from purple carrots to pink carrots on condition that you get carving knives.

Be flexible, dear diva, but make sure that you do not go below your Bottom Line. If you are getting close to your Bottom Line, it is time to take a breather and decide whether you want to continue with the deal or take it somewhere else.

Here are a few tips on giving and receiving proposals that will help you make the most of the proposals on the table.

## THREE TIPS FOR GIVING PROPOSALS
### 1. Present your proposal in a structured manner
Not only must the method in which you verbally communicate your proposal be structured, but the proposal itself needs to be clear and concise to have maximum

impact. Don't muddle up the 'If you' with explanations and justifications and the like. Keep the verbiage in check until after you have said the 'If you ... then I' part. Also ensure that the order of the proposal is correct – cabbage before chocolate.

## 2. Choose your words carefully

As you know, the actual words used in negotiating, particularly when you're making proposals, are critical. Success *is* in the semantics. Negotiation is about trading, and using the 'If you ... then I' format in your proposals helps to increase your control over the trading process.

## 3. Be specific when stating your conditions and making offers

Do not skimp on the details. Ensure that your conditions and offers are very clear – 'If you give me a discount of 12.3 per cent and thirty calendar days within which to pay, then I will sign the order next week Tuesday.' You should avoid being vague just as much as you should avoid being too wordy. Your proposals need to be short, sharp and specific.

## THREE TIPS FOR RECEIVING PROPOSALS

### 1. Listen, check that you've understood, ask questions

Make absolutely certain that you know *exactly* what you are being offered. Do not let assumptions go unchecked. Do not move forward until you have the detail – as much as you need to be specific when stating your conditions and offers, ascertain the same from the other party.

### 2. Never interrupt a proposal

Be as quiet as a church mouse. Keep your body and your eyes still. Listen and be in the moment. Remember the techniques for extracting sensitive information? Use them when you receive a proposal too. Maintain eye contact and keep quiet. You know those silly emails that go around saying that if you forward something to ten people you will receive a nice surprise? Well, in this case, even when they have finished presenting their proposal to you, be quiet and you will receive a nice

165

surprise – they will throw a yummy carrot or two at you to wake you up. Silence is golden.

### 3. Invite them to go dancing with you
I bet *that* got your attention!

### STRICTLY COME DANCING
Have you ever watched the television programme *Strictly Come Dancing*? If not, here's a brief explanation. A celebrity is paired with a professional dancer, and the dancer has to teach the celebrity to tango, foxtrot, waltz, rumba – you name it. Every week the couples have to perform in front of a panel of judges and the rubbish ones get tossed off the show. There is usually a tremendous improvement in the non-dancers' performances each week. I have watched only the BBC version, and my absolute favourite dancer of 2009 was the former boxing champion Joe Calzaghe. He looked like he had an ironing board strapped to his back and a carrot shoved up his oozlum.

Anyhow, a skilled dealmaker negotiating with an unskilled dealmaker is pretty much the same thing. The skilled dealmaker needs to help the unskilled dealmaker get to a deal. You can spot the unskilled guys really easily, because they:
– Are often aggressive or bullying.
– Don't seem to want do a deal.
– Keep saying 'no'.
– Make unreasonable demands.
– See trading as 'acting in bad faith'.
– Appear to pursue a win-lose strategy.
– Try to use negotiating tricks like 'good cop, bad cop'.
– Go round and round in circles – the Oozlum bird appears and disappears.

Picture the unskilled dealmaker as an unskilled dancer and you as the professional dancer. You need to take him in your arms and literally force him into a rhythm. You say, 'If you give me a package of R1 million per annum, I will accept the job of financial director.'

He says, 'Sorry, we can only offer you R800 000.'

You then take his clumsy move, the reduction to R800 000, and force it into an elegant step. 'Okay, if you give me the title of chief financial officer, a BMW 6 Series instead of a 5 Series, and you pay for one business-class ticket to America each year, then I will accept R800 000 per annum.'

He will say, 'We can't give you an overseas trip!'

You again take his lumbering move and twirl it around. 'If you give me the title of chief financial officer and the 6 Series, plus I get an extra five days' annual leave, I will accept R800 000 per year.' It is exactly the same process as trading the pink and purple carrots.

Every time he takes an awkward step, you guide him into a more graceful movement. It is impossible to do this without your pre-prepared Marbles.

Dancing with an unskilled dealmaker takes a lot more time and effort than dancing with a skilled one. You might be thinking that you'd rather negotiate with someone who is unskilled, but this actually makes for a rather difficult life. A skilled dealmaker will not usually try to take advantage of you – they understand value for value, and the consequences of being greedy.

Do you know the essential difference between a skilled and an unskilled dealmaker? When Robert 'Bobby' Godsell (*South African businessman and former chairman of Eskom; 1952–*) was the chief negotiator for Anglo American Gold Division, he had to negotiate with the National Union of Mineworkers (NUM – the most radical union in its day). In an interview, he was asked what made him such a successful negotiator. His reply? 'I give them what they want.' Godsell was saying that the difference between him and an unskilled dealmaker is his ability to give the other party what they want, and for him, in return, to get what he wants. If NUM demanded a 40 per cent pay hike, he would probably say something along the lines of, 'If you give me a 40 per cent increase in productivity, I will give you a 40 per cent wage increase.' I guess the Eskom board had a severe case of two left feet.

Give me a skilled negotiator any day – they understand the rules of the game:

give to get, quid pro quo, something for something, trading. The only time skilled negotiators will push a deal to their absolute benefit is when it is a once-off, short-term transaction.

How, though, does one manage an unskilled dealmaker?
- Allocate more time to the deal.
- Tango with them!
- Avoid debate and stick to trading.
- Understand that they are ego-driven and will want to 'win'.
- Use lots of summaries to chase off the Oozlum bird.
- Tie down the deal in detail.

## WHEN SOMEONE SAYS 'NO'

There will be times when, no matter how hard you persuade, how well you prepare or how reasonable you think you are being, the other party will say 'no'. What's a girl to do? Actually, there are a number of things you can try.

In the movie *Love Actually*, Hugh Grant, playing the British prime minister, meets with Billy Bob Thornton (the American president). Billy Bob says to the prime minister, 'I'll give you anything you ask for as long as it's not something I don't want to give.' As silly as this may sound, people do go into negotiations already having decided that they will not give the other party *x* for whatever reason. This is usually because of where they have drawn the Bottom Line of their Ball Park, or they are playing a power game – commonly called 'being a clever clog'.

Try to find out *why* they are being inflexible. If you can't get an answer (below are a few ideas on how to extract the information), or you realise that they are merely taking a stand, try to change their minds by persuading them of the benefits in shifting their position. However, if you are not able to convince them without a fight, your next step is to establish where they *are* prepared to be flexible. You then go back to *your* Ball Park and adjust it to accommodate what you have learnt about their needs. Try to give them what they want, but only in exchange for exactly what *you* want. Just because you pre-prepared your Ball Park doesn't mean that you have to live or die by the original plan. Be flexible; get creative.

As Jim Morrison wrote, 'People are strange.' The other party might not want to give you the reasons for their position, or why they are rejecting your proposals, but here are some killer questions that you can use to test their boundaries:
- What do I need to do to get you to agree to my proposal?
- What must I change to make my proposal acceptable to you?
- Exactly what is it in my proposal that you find unacceptable?
- On what conditions will you give me what I want?
- Can you give me a detailed response to each line of my proposal?
- If I do $x$ for you, will you do $y$ for me?
- What if I were to change $x$ part of my proposal?
- Just suppose I were to offer you $y$?

You, dear diva, presumably do not want to be the unskilled dealmaker flailing around on the dance floor with someone else forcing you into elegant moves. You want to be the lovely lead dancer, don't you? For that to happen, you need to follow Bobby Godsell's advice: Give them what they want. Oh, *and* get exactly what you are after in return! Don't say 'no'; say, 'If you do this for me, then I will give you what you want.'

Interesting fact this: I have never seen an expert dealmaker say 'no'. Even if the other party wants something completely outrageous, the expert just makes sure that she gets something equally outrageous in return. This usually has the effect of seeing off the ridiculous demand. Imagine an employer tells you that, if you want the promotion you have been chasing, you must put in an eighty-hour week every week for one year to show your commitment. Sounds like blackmail, doesn't it?

Your likely answer would be: 'No, don't be ridiculous. I deserve my promotion and I am not prepared to live in my office.' But how would the lead dancer deal with this? She would say, 'If you are prepared to buy me an apartment very close to the office, give me the promotion immediately and pay me double my rate for anything over sixty hours a week, I would be happy to agree to your terms.' Who has the problem now? You are prepared to do what the other person says, but at such a huge price that it transfers the problem to *them*.

Here's another example: A prospective customer was stalling on giving me a large order. I knew that the big bosses were happy with the deal, but their head of learning and development was holding back on signing the agreement. I went to meet with him and demanded to know what his problem was. 'Kim,' he said, 'if you wear a very short skirt the next time you come in, I'll sign the order.' This is bullsh*t, I thought, but I had two choices: I could prostitute myself and wear the short skirt, or I could go over his head and make a scene.

I phoned him the next day to set up the appointment to sign the deal. I arrived in the most minuscule mini ever. I got the order – and the lunch at the South African president's personal restaurant in the Union Buildings that I had demanded. How could I sell out and wear the mini? I figured that, if I wore the skirt and didn't get the order, I would at least know that this man was going to be a problem and that I would need to work directly with the bosses. As it turned out, he was delighted with my mini – he had been teasing me, thinking I was just a humourless Driver chick. To this day we have a great relationship – and he has never, not once, acted improperly.

## TO WALK AWAY OR NOT TO WALK AWAY?

A question you might be itching to ask is whether it is ever appropriate to throw in the towel. As I've said, I have never seen expert dealmakers walk away. Their ability to give the other party what they want keeps the deal moving forward, even in very trying circumstances. The other factor that the *experts* have in common is that they take emotion out of a negotiation. For them, it's never personal. We are talking about experts, though.

Here are three situations when you may choose not to do the deal:

1. Remember the *Indecent Proposal* exercise we did? I encouraged you to see everything, including your values and morals, as 'negotiable'. I did say, though, that it depended on the price you would have to pay to get what you want. Please, please, please – I beg you not to see things as 'negotiable' or 'not negotiable', but if somebody asks you for something that goes against every fibre of your being, you might choose to walk away and keep your integrity intact. Your call.

2. When someone else – like your boss or even your spouse – has set the mandate (including the Marbles) and determined the Bottom Line, you need to either renegotiate your mandate or walk away if the other party wants you to drop below your total package limit. Expert negotiators do not always have a 'Bottom Line' – they know their issues, have a zillion Marbles and understand the exact value they want from the negotiation for each issue. Lesser mortals do need to define the deal in detail, but … no Marbles = no flexibility = no trophy for dance champion.
3. This last situation requires good judgement. If doing the deal with the other party is excruciating, every single move is a struggle and you're not sure you actually want to work with this type of person, consider walking away. It is *very* difficult for someone who can smell the deal to stop and take stock, but this is exactly what you might need to do. If the other party has shown any dishonesty, mistrust or the likelihood of reneging on what has been agreed, the deal is going to be a full-on bitch by the time it gets to the implementation stage.

Distinguish between when you *need* to walk away and when you are simply making excuses for giving up because the going is getting too tough. If you throw in the towel too easily, you don't get to experience the enormous high of a hard job done well. If, for good reason, you do throw in the towel, don't punish yourself. Giving up is difficult, so the last thing you need is a beating. Pick yourself up, shake yourself off and start preparing for the next round.

There are people with whom I *choose* not to engage, as I feel we do not share a common set of values – and trust me, I am very flexible! One or two people I will even cross the road to avoid; it's almost as if being in their space contaminates my soul. There are also a few companies with which I will not work; their culture is so foul that just the thought of them makes me nauseous. These are the deals from which I choose to walk away.

## GUIDELINES FOR ENGAGEMENT

Back to the deals we *want* to do. There are *three rules* you should follow to ensure that your negotiating encounter gives you what you want. Remember, though, always to try to persuade first – only negotiate if you can't convince the other person to give you what you want unconditionally.

The 'Three Rules of Trading' in a negotiation are:
1. **Trade:** To get, you have to give.
2. **Trade everything:** You need lots of trading variables – Marbles – with which to trade.
3. **Trade everything wisely:** To get what *you* want, give them what *they* really want.

## WHEN ENOUGH IS ENOUGH

You will sense when you are coming to the close of the negotiation – the Key Issues will be more or less finalised and you will be fiddling around with the Marbles. It's time to stop the trading. Enough is enough. Closure is what we are after – so here is the last tiny mouthful of the elephant-sized definition:

> Dealmaker: A person skilled in using instinct, processes and expertise in primarily negotiation, selling and communication, and able to leverage or adjust the balance of power **to bring closure to transactions that usually benefit all parties.**
>
> © The Dealmaker Programmes Company

Jean Paul 'J.P.' Getty Sr (*American industrialist and billionaire; 1892–1976*) once insightfully remarked: 'My father said: "You must never try to make all the money that's in a deal. Let the other fellow make some money too, because if you have a reputation for always making all the money, you won't have many deals."' Do not get greedy – don't try to scalp the deal. Recognise when you have enough and when the value-for-value quotient is fair, and then tell the other party that it is time to close the deal.

When we discussed 'power' earlier, there were two additional sources of power that I held back for the 'how' section. One was the *power of proposals*, which we have now covered, and the other is the *power of closing*, which is our final learning point.

There is considerable power in closing a deal properly. Do not neglect this stage of the negotiation. 'How' should you close the deal? There are *five simple steps* you need to follow.

## FIVE STEPS TO CLOSING THE DEAL
### Step 1: Tell them that you want to close the deal
When you see the Marbles coming into play and you're happy with the value-value in the deal, say to the other side, 'I think we have a deal. If you agree, let's close off here, without putting anything further on the table.' This statement not only clearly signals the end of the trading, but it has the added benefit that if the other party has any hidden-agenda items, they either have to put them on the table or let them go. It is better to know now whether there are any secrets lurking in the closet than to find out, after you think you've done the deal, that you need to start from scratch again.

### Step 2: Double-check the deal
Before you shake hands, double-check that all the agenda items have been addressed and compare the deal you are about to sign to your Likely position. If you realise that you've made a mistake or need to adjust something, now is the time to do it. Do not try to sneak anything into the agreement, as you will probably ruin the whole deal *and* damage the relationship. Rather say to the other side that there is 'just one last thing I need to discuss', and put it on the table. Be aware that this is liable to reopen the negotiation, which is still better than signing a deal you will regret.

This is also the point at which you will bring in the Expert Advisors and big bosses if you need their input or approval. Don't exclude them unnecessarily, as having them test and validate the deal can be extremely useful.

Tie down the detail and close any loopholes – you do not want any surprises later. If you are bad with detail (you are probably an Expressive or Amiable), get someone to help you with this – i.e. a Vice-captain who is an Analytical.

### Step 3: Finalise the deal

When you are sure that everything is on the table and that no further adjustments need to be made, check that both parties understand the deal. This is particularly important when you are working with different cultures or in different languages. Two people can glean completely different meanings from the same word. How should you check? Summarise their side, summarise your side, summarise the whole deal and summarise again. Bored? Then get someone to do this part of the deal for you. Just because you don't want to handle the detail doesn't mean it shouldn't be done. Closing is the stage at which you thank heaven for Analyticals.

### Step 4: Close the deal

Once you have tested and confirmed that both parties understand the detail of the deal, agree on the implementation process – who does what, when, where. Then put everything in writing in a contract, email, fax or minutes – whatever form is appropriate to the deal. *Nothing* should be left out. Details have a habit of mutating into an unrecognisable form if you leave them alone for too long.

### Step 5: Sign the deal

Ideally, you want to sign the deal there and then. That's the purpose of a document like 'Heads of Agreement'. 'Heads' are signed while everything is still fresh in everyone's minds, before a contract is drafted. Even a handwritten piece of paper will do – anything is better than nothing.

Making a deal, as Dr Peter Drucker said, is exciting and fun. But it is all too easy to get swept up in the euphoria of the moment and neglect the detail of the deal. This can have disastrous consequences. Early on in my selling and negotiating career, I 'signed' a fabulous deal with a large global consulting company for a three-year training project. It was a Friday afternoon and I was ecstatic. The customer shook my hand and said we would sign all the contracts the following week.

That very weekend I went to Cape Town with my man to celebrate, and we returned as the owners (rather unexpectedly) of a house in Hout Bay. We are as bad as each other when it comes to spontaneously buying big-ticket items! That same weekend, the customer was tragically killed in a car accident. I never did get to close the deal – the detail died with the customer. Simon had to bail me out of my financial commitments in Hout Bay and, in return, I had to give him my share of the house.

## HOW TO WOO FRIENDS AND WIN FAMILY

Talking about doing deals with loved ones, as an oozlum-kicking negotiator it's important not to lose all your friends or alienate your family along the way. When you start trading with them, they will be surprised (to say the least) when something you happily gave them in the past now has a price tag attached to it. Here are few tips on how to keep the loved ones happy.

You need to decide where you will continue to give unconditionally and where you will want value in return. I would suggest that getting something in exchange for giving your man a birthday present is a little hectic. Unless it's … hmmm, let's not go there. Santa, of course, is not supposed to bring presents to children who have been naughty!

It's the day-to-day expectations that will present the challenge. For example, when you get home this evening and your partner wants you to feed the dog, water the plants or make dinner, do you retort with, 'Well, if you take me out for dinner, I'll feed Rufus'? This is far more likely to provoke an argument than get you a dinner. Plan your strategy more carefully. When he comes home, you might want to gently 'suggest' that you will cook his favourite meal for him tomorrow night if he takes you out for dinner tonight. If he wants you to cook it tonight, say that you need to shop for ingredients tomorrow, but would he mind feeding the dog while you get ready to go out? It's worth a try. It generally works for me – except the cooking bit. I promise something else!

There are times – and loved ones are a case in point – when you may want to give something, or do something for somebody, out of the generosity of your heart. Go ahead and do it. Be very careful of saying, 'I was being generous', when what you were really doing was being a negotiating wimp or avoiding trading.

Do not pretend, like a delegate did on a recent course, that because you adore your customers you can give without expecting anything in return. The golden rule in dealmaking is always to make sure that there is a value-for-value exchange! With family, it's love.

## ON GETTING YOUR OWN WAY

My wicked diva friends, who have contributed so generously to this book, insisted that I include this story about not walking away or giving in during a personal negotiation.

One of the things I enjoy about travelling with newly founded airlines is that, if you fly business class, they don't fuss too much about the weight of your luggage. I checked in with such an airline last summer, my outward-bound suitcases weighing forty-two kilograms. My philosophy on travelling light is that it's the most ridiculous notion – what if you suddenly need your red kitten-heel boots? It was a very sad day for the world when steam travel, passenger liners and professional luggage-carriers became outdated.

Anyhow, the check-in clerk informed me that I would have to pay for nine kilograms of excess baggage. I was outraged. I was incredulous. I feigned shock. I even argued about the unfairness of thin people having the same baggage allowance as obese travellers. I finally threatened to empty my bags and put on all my clothes – which I promptly started doing.

Making no headway and wearing three extra coats, I stomped off to the excess-baggage counter to start a new fight. On finding out that I had to pay nearly R3 000, I ceremoniously unpacked my bags, spread my stuff about the departures hall, crammed as much as I could into my hand luggage and went back to the check-in counter to tell them I did not need to pay the excess as I was, miraculously, much lighter.

By now the extra clothing – along with two large suitcases, a computer trolley, a handbag and an armful of shoes – was causing me to sweat, and the fuss I was creating had attracted the attention of the duty manager. I suggested to him that, if he allowed me the additional baggage on the trip out, he could deduct the excess weight from my return-journey allowance. He stared at me like I was a mad person. I pointed out to him that my bags were now only thirty-six kilograms. So, giving me the 10 per cent leeway, I was really only three kilograms overweight. He finally grimaced and nodded to the check-in lady.

My *coup de grâce* was trying to return the stuff I was holding and wearing back into my checked cases before the conveyor belt took them away from me. Oy, what a protest. I had to carry my excess baggage on my person! Can you believe it? I managed to get through security (four full trays) and immigration uneventfully, before going into a shop, buying biltong for our nephews and begging for a huge carrier bag. I boarded the plane looking like a bag lady.

My lesson? I need to work harder to keep the tradition of travelling heavy alive. I will not surrender!

# Chapter 9

## REAL-LIFE DEAL DIVAS

> 'There is a special place in hell for women who do not help other women.' – *Madeleine K. Albright*
> *(American politician and professor; 1937–)*

It has been both my privilege and my pleasure to be exposed to some of the world's best dealmakers. I have watched, worked with and been guided by them. I have participated in their deals and done deals, big and small, on my own. Rather immodestly, I think I'm a pretty good negotiator (even if I'm not a guru quite yet). But, in order to double-check my perceptions on the subject, I thought it would be a sound idea to interview a few of South Africa's top female dealmakers to get their perspectives on negotiating.

As I said in Chapter 2, when I started doing the research for this book, I was sure that the reason women do not get the same deals as men – in business and in life – was that they aren't as good at negotiating as men. It was as I interviewed the fabulous *femmes* in this chapter that I noticed four patterns that were at odds with my original views and research. I realised that:

1. Successful women – whether in business or at home – *do* know how to negotiate.
2. Women who lack confidence or experience are usually poor negotiators.

3. Women with a victim or doormat mentality – a mindset of scarcity rather than abundance – are routinely the worst negotiators.
4. Women value themselves differently from men.

With the honesty of hindsight, I think the questions I posed to the top female deal-makers during the interviews were unintentionally skewed to support my theories. You can imagine my surprise when I discovered that I – a Leo, a Driver – was *wrong*. I will include the questions I asked where appropriate, but these fantastic women shared so much more than just answers. They shared their stories.

Rather than consolidating the interviews, there is a section dedicated to each person so that you can get a 'feel' for who they are and what they think is important at an individual level. The order below corresponds with the order in which I interviewed the women. You will notice that the format gradually changes as I start moving away from asking the prescribed questions towards their personal stories.

My profound and heartfelt thanks to Shaz Maxwell for making my life so much easier and typing up the notes from the interviews. Not only did Shaz add quality input during the actual interviews, but her insights and observations afterwards were invaluable in helping me to formulate the essence of my thinking. Shaz, you are a real diva, darling.

## JOAN JOFFE

Joan Joffe is South African born, holds a BA degree in mathematics and logic from the University of the Witwatersrand, and studied computer science at Stanford University in the United States.

One of the very few women in the early information technology (IT) industry, Joan started her own IT company, Joffe Associates, in 1977 and sold it, ten years later, to Datakor Ltd. It was in that same year – 1987 – that Joan was voted Businesswoman of the Year.

After leaving Datakor, Joan assumed an executive role at Vodacom Ltd, a position she held for ten years. She was also the first chairman of the Vodacom Foundation.

Joan currently runs her own IT and telecoms consultancy and serves on the boards of several companies.

Joan and I originally met when Datakor bought Joffe Associates in 1987. Joan, through immense generosity of spirit, became my informal mentor. She took the time to gently point me in the right direction when she thought it would help, and always made herself available to guide me when I was dazed and confused.

Joan is an entrepreneur and a self-made woman. She is an Analytical, but she can be quite Expressive when she is passionate about a subject. Joan is also a networker of the highest order – she seems to know everyone!

### Do women get the same deal in business as men?

Joan has never felt disadvantaged as a woman in business, which she attributes to the fact that she has always chosen the road contrary to the one dictated by convention. She chose to study at a time when women were conditioned to get married, have babies and serve their husbands.

Joan believes that if you are told something often enough (such as you are not mathematically inclined, can't negotiate or are not artistic) it lodges itself in the unconscious and translates into what you accept about yourself, which ultimately impacts your self-worth. If a woman thinks she can't expect to earn the same as a man, for whatever reason, then she will earn less.

Being a natural rebel, Joan rejected this pre-programming. It never occurred to her that she could not achieve something once she'd set her mind to it. She defines success as 'the achievement of your own personal goals'. However, she emphasises that an important part of success is down to a person's drive, hard work and knowledge – you need to know everything there is to know about your particular business if you want to be taken seriously.

Joan feels it is important to understand that not every woman wants to be chief executive, just as not everybody wants to be president of the United States. In exploring this line of thought with Joan, she raised a very interesting question: Did Hillary Clinton fail to win the Democratic nomination because she is a woman, or did she simply not have the same powers of persuasion as Barack Obama?

## What can women do to improve the deals they get in business?

It is critical to have other options available to you when you negotiate. Joan believes that having an alternative position (what the gurus call 'BATNA' – a **B**est **A**lternative **T**o a **N**egotiated **A**greement – similar to our catalogues of choices) gave her power when she was negotiating with IBM many years ago. For those of you who don't know, Joan brought the very first personal computer into South Africa – well before IBM itself, or any other computer company, for that matter. When IBM refused to service the computers Joan was importing into the country, she obtained the technical specifications of the products and serviced them herself. While she blew up a few units during the learning process, Joan says, this solution ultimately gave her a critical advantage in business.

Women should not see gender differences as a hindrance. There were virtually no women in the IT industry in 1977, and Joan found this a great advantage. She was always able to get appointments and never had a door slammed in her face. Joan says she secured her first appointment with Anglo American purely because she was a novelty – a woman in a man's world. Anglo American went on to become one of Joan's most important customers. Joan suggests that women have an advantage precisely because they bring diversity to the workplace – they think and behave differently from men. Women have no need to imitate men. Just being themselves and using the differences between the genders, without compromising their principles, allows women to do well in business.

Women previously lost out on certain deals because they lacked the opportunity to network, such as on the golf course or at the 'club', but this is changing – to the benefit of women. It also helps that the 'old school tie' is starting to disappear. Another positive change is that women have become more supportive of each other in business, which was certainly not the case early on in Joan's career!

## Top tips to help women improve their negotiating skills
1. Approach a deal with confidence – know what you want and set your limits. If you are not feeling confident, don't let it show. Don't blink!
2. Give yourself options – have alternatives so that you are not forced to do a deal

that does not offer you what you want. Be in a position to take the deal somewhere else.
3. Deals done in desperation are not good deals. Don't be afraid to walk away if it is not a deal beneficial to both parties.
4. Do your homework. Research the personality styles involved in the negotiation and get all the facts and figures you might need. Strategise.
5. Be professional. Do not let your emotions get in the way.
6. Treat the other party with respect. Allow them to keep their dignity.

You now have a little insight into why Joan Joffe is one of the doyennes of the IT world, both in South Africa and abroad.

## KATE RAU

After obtaining her degree at the University of Johannesburg, Kate Rau worked as a journalist. At the age of twenty-three, she was already an editor. By her own admission, Kate is very competitive.

She has been involved in the magazine world for eight years and has been editor of *SALESGURU* for the last two years.

Although I knew Kate by reputation, we had not met before the interview. I did not expect the editor of a magazine to be so young – it was a very pleasant surprise indeed.

Kate is a Driver, and I can imagine her becoming very Expressive when she's in an animated mood.

### Do women get the same deal in business as men?

Kate thinks the disparity in earnings comes about because, more often than not, men make the salary decisions and they are not aware of the effort women put into their positions, particularly when it comes to the detail a job entails.

Women are not inclined to ask for what they want, says Kate. This leads men to think that women in business are not tough enough and, as a result, men do not take them seriously. Similarly to the other divas, Kate believes that women should be prepared to use their feminine charm to help them get what they want in business. As Kate remarked, 'We use our powers of persuasion very successfully at home with our partners'!

**What can women do to improve the deals they get in business?**
Kate does not think that women are such poor negotiators; it's just that their approach and motivation are different from that of men. If, say, a woman is negotiating a salary increase, she finds it necessary to justify, in detail, why she should be paid more. A man, on the other hand, simply says he needs more money and asks for the increase.

Through her work with *SALESGURU*, Kate has noticed that South Africans have allowed price to become their main negotiating tool. She observes that, in the overseas market, price is only one part of a deal being negotiated. Kate believes that this is an area in which women have an advantage over men with their negotiating skills – they can move away from price and focus on the *value* of a deal.

Like Graça Machel, who feels that young people today have virtually stopped fighting for what they believe to be fair and right, Kate suggests that women fought much harder in years gone by to get what they wanted. But, she says, women are better at bonding with one another in business than they used to be, although they don't use their connections enough.

When I discussed the support women give each other in business with Nicola Coetzer, a beautiful blonde bombshell with a razor-sharp mind and a heart of gold (and one of the youngest partners at a leading South African legal firm), she endorsed Kate's views. Nicola believes that women are better at supporting each other now than they were in the past, and that they are actually pleased when there is another woman on a project or in a team. Older women far more readily mentor their younger counterparts than used to be the case, but the claws still come out occasionally when women have to compete with each other in business.

Nicola thinks that the days of the power-suited super-bitch are over, but that there is still some way to go before women support each other in business in the same automatic way that men do. Women are far better at getting what they want from men than from other women, though, which Nicola attributes to feminine wiles working better on the boys.

Catie Louw, another gorgeous young blonde, is the director of equity derivative sales in global markets at Standard Bank, and she agrees with both Nicola and Kate that women in business today do seem more encouraging of each other. Catie is not sure whether this is a fundamental shift or a reflection of the culture in which she works, but her experience of supportive women has been extremely positive.

In a recent effort to improve her work–life balance, Catie wanted to change her working conditions without compromising her position or her responsibilities. She was unsure how this change would be received in the workplace, considering that she is a director and has a team that reports directly to her. Catie was delighted to be given advice and coaching from a senior female executive. This guidance helped Catie to solicit the conditional approval of her boss.

The next obstacle was to secure the buy-in of her team. Catie was concerned about the younger women's reaction, but instead she was overwhelmed by their support. She is not sure that she would have achieved her objectives without the assistance of her female work colleagues.

Although most of her mentors are male, Catie recognises that women relate to each other on a number of levels, which she does not find with male colleagues. Women, says Catie, are much stronger when they are on the same team rather than competing head-on!

**Top tips from Kate to help women improve their negotiating skills**
1. Pay more attention to how you value yourself. If you don't acknowledge your own value, nobody else will.
2. Stop feeling you have to justify your salary expectations. If a company is doing badly, a woman won't ask for an increase; not so with a man. Just ask, and let the company decide if it wants to give you the increase or not.
3. Women must do business like women, not like men. Being true to your gender will serve you better.

4. Women can get too bogged down in the detail, whereas men keep the big picture in mind.

Shaz and I were delighted when Kate said, 'If you really want the job to be done, give it to a woman.'

## ELIZABETH MALUMO

Zambian-born Elizabeth Malumo entered university to study medicine but, after her first frog dissection, beat a hasty retreat. Her disappointed father happened to be having drinks with the local bank manager that night and he mentioned that his daughter needed a job. The next day Elizabeth presented herself at the local branch of the bank.

In 1984 Elizabeth joined Meridien Bank, where she gained experience in a number of departments, and when First National Bank (FNB) bought Meridien, she moved to international banking. Soon finding herself bored and restless, Elizabeth negotiated a salary cut and became a trainee manager in credit management. During this time she gained a qualification from the Institute of Bankers.

During 1993, Elizabeth spent six months in the United States after being selected for a professional development programme. She spent weekdays working at JP Morgan and Saturdays at university.

Today, Elizabeth is the only female regional director of FNB, and is the founder of FNB's Women in Business Forum. This women's forum is where I first met Elizabeth. I was knocked out by her style, glamour and poise.

Elizabeth, a corporate woman, is an Expressive, with a healthy dose of Amiable.

### Do women get the same attention in business as men?
Elizabeth feels that women don't sell themselves properly in business. This is a result of a stereotypical upbringing. The best way in which a woman can overcome this obstacle is to be as technically competent as she can about her industry and company, and to not be afraid to get into detailed discussions. Elizabeth believes

that women should gather the information they need by asking the right people the right questions. 'Do your homework, network and listen,' is her advice.

When asked how she came to the attention of Dr Michael Jordaan (read all about him in *Work Diva*), who is the chief executive officer of FNB, Elizabeth says that she took the initiative. She simply went up to Michael and introduced herself, and proceeded to tell him about the changes she would like to see made in the bank. Soon after this bold move, Michael invited Elizabeth to an executive lunch to explore her views. It was there that he learnt she'd done national service in Zambia and that she was able to strip and reassemble a rifle.

Elizabeth takes pride and pleasure in developing other people, especially women. She encourages them to be true to themselves and their dreams. She feels that women should not compromise on their values or be afraid to speak out. In order to do so, women need to have both self-respect and respect for the dignity of others.

**What roles do culture, gender and race play in business?**
Elizabeth believes that, although most companies have good policies and procedures in place, actual practices do not always align with the policies.

She thinks that cultural backgrounds and levels of education do affect the way in which black males perceive black women in business. In Elizabeth's experience, black males brought up in single-parent families, where there has been no male role model, are far more open-minded about working women than those brought up in more traditional homes.

In 1996, when Elizabeth was appointed customer services manager at a Johannesburg branch of the bank, she was handed a portfolio consisting of predominantly conservative white men. They refused to acknowledge a black woman as the manager and decision-maker, but with the support of her boss (a white male), Elizabeth stood her ground and refused to take the slight personally. She treated her male customers as she did everyone else – with fairness, firmness and courtesy – and so slowly won their respect, and even their support. What you need to know, dear diva, is that Elizabeth is a *very* charming woman.

## Top tips to help women improve their negotiating skills
1. Make sure that you understand who you are and always be true to yourself.
2. Set clear boundaries for the negotiation. Tell the other party what you want and then be prepared to negotiate up or down, but always be specific and detailed.
3. You need to be able to defend your expectations. You must have the facts to back up your proposal.
4. Be clear about what you want and communicate how you expect to be treated. Allow others to save face.
5. Business and emotion are intertwined, but don't be afraid to take time out if a business decision is being affected by your emotions. Men see an emotional outburst as a weakness.

Never mind all her other accomplishments, the fact that Elizabeth could dismantle and reassemble an FN rifle impressed the hell out of Shaz and me.

## JENNA CLIFFORD
South African Jenna Clifford grew up in one of the poorer suburbs of Johannesburg (coincidentally the same area in which I was born). Jenna, like Joan Joffe, is a self-made entrepreneur and a national icon. She is the founding member, designer and a director of Jenna Clifford (Pty) Ltd, which was launched in 1992.

In 2000 Jenna orchestrated the successful amalgamation of three women's business forums – the Executive Women's Club, ProWaldo and the National Association of Women Business Owners (NAWBO) – to form the Businesswomen's Association (BWA). De Leeuw Roses named a rose after her, with all royalties from sales donated to the BWA.

In August 2008, Jenna was appointed as one of three South African ambassadors and torchbearers for the United Nations Millennium Development Goals 3: Call to Action Global Campaign, which draws attention to the empowerment of women and gender equality. She shares this honour with Archbishop Emeritus Desmond

Tutu and the Soweto Gospel Choir. Jenna was a nominated finalist in the Ernst & Young World Entrepreneur Awards in 2008 as one of five emerging world-seasoned entrepreneurs, and she was the recipient of Rentmeester/Rapport's Most Inspirational and Beautiful Woman of South Africa award in 1997 and the CEO Top Women in Business award in 2007.

Jenna is a committed philanthropist. Dream Big is a powerful initiative inspired by Jenna and Olympic gold medallist Ryk Neethling to 'unite and harness the dual power of genders and instil a visionary, balanced and prosperous society that "dreams big"!' Dream Big supports the WSPCCA (Walter Sisulu Paediatric and Cardiac Centre for Africa) as well as the Tomorrow Trust. A percentage of proceeds from all Dream Big items sold goes to these children's organisations.

Jenna is an Expressive, with a bit more Expressive, so seeing her lecture is an outrageous and riveting treat. I met her when we were both presenting at a Women's Day function in 2009 and was struck by her warmth, sincerity, generosity and *joie de vivre*.

And, as an Expressive, Jenna wanted to discuss the big picture – things of much greater importance to women and the world than just negotiating. I was completely absorbed and humbled by the route the discussion took.

### Do women get the same deal in business, and in life, as men?

Jenna feels women have had only an inkling of success. Like Joan Joffe, she believes that the historic rendering on their psyche means that only 3 to 5 per cent of women have overcome societal suppression and risen to the top of their chosen fields. Because women do not value themselves as they should, and because of their previous conditioning, they do not ask for what they want.

Jenna says women have a scarcity mentality, and suggests that they need to shift to a mindset of abundance. She also thinks legislation should protect and grow women in business and society and, once in place, that this legislation should be enforced. Unfortunately, in societies where there is a gross violation of the 'system' (in South Africa, for example, the lack of respect for the rule of law), the enforcement of such nurturing policies becomes almost impossible.

Jenna asserts that women are subjugated in the workplace and that this practice must stop. Men need to realise that women are the essence of the new order. But it's not just the men that need to change their behaviour. Jenna thinks women must become far more proactive in taking the gap to make their mark in the new order.

And we do *need* a new order – Jenna cited these terrifying statistics in a recent interview with Erica Webster of *Business Day*:

> Women constitute about 54% of the world's population, yet inequality persists in many arenas. More than 110 million of the world's children, two thirds of them girls, are not in school. Of the world's 875 million illiterate adults, two thirds are women. Domestic violence is the leading cause of injury and death for women worldwide. The statistics are particularly frightening in South Africa, which has the world's highest reported rates of rape. Most South African rapists go unpunished because it is one of the most under-reported crimes and because it has one of the lowest conviction rates.

Men divide and conquer, while women, despite all their power as birthers, abdicate their responsibility to stop the destruction. Women need to use passive resistance to bring about change, and should direct their businesses and money to those enterprises that do no further damage to the planet – even when it comes to choosing a dentist! Women, after all, are the most powerful consumers! They should use all the tools at their disposal – their voice, the internet, purchasing power – to make sure that their message demanding change is heard.

Jenna, who has experienced abuse at the hands of men, is quick to point out that not all men are aggressive or abusive. She sees a whole new group of positive male role models coming through, such as Ryk Neethling (yum #3). She also believes that men like Thabo Mbeki have done a tremendous amount to promote gender equality and empowerment, and that this should be celebrated.

The answer, Jenna believes, lies with the 'crystal children' (born 2000 onwards), who are going to change the world. Combine these children with the growing breed of women who are recognising the importance of sustaining the planet, and the cavemen are in for a rude awakening. 'God has given us all a lot of opportunity, a beautiful planet and life,' says Jenna. 'It's up to all of us to set a new way forward, especially in this enlightened age. Nothing ever comes without hard work, determination, perseverance and love. You have to have those things in your heart.'

Amen, Jenna. May your role as a custodian of the earth be supported by everyone who hears your name and whose lives you touch. I'm in.

## PROFESSOR SHIRLEY ZINN

Shirley Zinn was born and raised on the Cape Flats in Cape Town – another less than salubrious area. Shirley realised at a young age that she wanted more for herself than a life on 'the Flats'.

Her first corporate position was with Southern Life as training manager, but she soon moved into senior management. She became the executive head for employment equity at Computer Configurations Holdings, then director of 'special programmes' at the Department of Public Service and Administration. From there she moved on to become regional human resources director for the Middle East and Africa for Reckitt Benckiser, and then general manager for human resources at the South African Revenue Service (SARS).

Shirley is currently director of human resources at Nedbank. She is also an extraordinary professor at the University of Pretoria's department of human resource management, and chairperson of the Institute of Bankers. She serves as a board member for both BANKSETA and Monash University in South Africa.

Shirley holds a BA degree, a higher diploma in education from the University of the Western Cape (UWC), a BEd (Hons) from UNISA and a master's degree in education from UWC. *And*, divas, she has both a master's degree and a PhD from Harvard University. Shirley's doctoral thesis was on anti-racist teacher education.

Shirley, whom I had not had the pleasure of spending time with before the interview, is probably a Driver, with a secondary style of Analytical.

Shirley's story was so compelling that Shaz and I completely forgot to focus on negotiation (as you will see).

## What lessons have driven Shirley's success and how did these come about?

Shirley believes that *education is a key pillar* in any democracy, and that no country can grow if it does not educate its people. When Shirley discussed with her parents her desire to attend university, they, although supportive, were concerned that the family could not afford to lose her potential income. According to Shirley, she was not a natural 'A-grade' student, but she worked hard to achieve good results, which helped her to secure a government bursary.

After obtaining her master's degree at UWC, she was selected for the Harvard/South Africa Fellowship, and spent a year studying in Boston. When she discovered that she would be required to do a second master's degree before she could start her PhD at Harvard, Shirley and her husband Kevin sold all their possessions and double-bonded their house to raise the funds she needed to complete her studies. She reflects that her greatest lesson from this period of hardship is accepting that there are times in life when you *simply have to take risks*.

On returning to South Africa from the United States, Shirley realised that Cape Town was not the place where she could achieve her vision of making a difference to the lives of others, and she and her husband moved to Pretoria.

Soon afterwards, Shirley and Kevin were involved in a devastating car accident in which their young son, Jamie, lost his life. Shirley spent six months recovering from her own injuries, and when she returned to work, she found that her heart was no longer in her job. She needed to be with people who would help her to heal. She firmly believes that when you need it, *you must have the courage to ask for help*.

It took a while, but when Shirley started to feel whole once more, she joined SARS. It wasn't long, however, before Tom Boardman, then chief executive officer of Nedbank, approached Shirley to join the bank. Although Shirley did not want to leave SARS so soon after joining, she reflects today that she is pleased she made the move, as she has been able to make a significant contribution to the people in the company and the roles they play at Nedbank.

Like Jenna Clifford, Shirley believes considerable discrimination against women still exists, but that *women need to take responsibility* for overcoming any obstacles in life if they want to live the life they deserve.

**Top tips to help women improve their negotiating skills**
1. Be authentically you – live your values.
2. Never give up on the vision you have for your life.
3. Setbacks and disappointments are part of the journey and help you to realise who you truly are, and who you are meant to be.
4. Be passionate, determined, organised – and surround yourself with people who inspire you.
5. You can make the impossible possible.

Shaz and I were incredibly moved by Shirley's story and the hardships she's had to endure in her life, especially the loss of her beloved son Jamie. Shirley has incredible presence and is exquisitely groomed, but we both felt her sadness.

**TERRY DEARLING**
Terry Dearling is another successful South African businesswoman who started out on the less desirable side of the tracks (in her case, Springs). Her father convinced her to get a degree, and she graduated with a BA in psychology from the University of the Witwatersrand. Terry credits her father with having far more belief in her than she had in herself.

Terry describes her early career as 'unfocused' (I think she's just being modest). After what she describes as 'a disastrous start with a personnel agency', Terry joined Babcock Engineering. A year later, she moved to Medscheme as personnel manager – a move that afforded her the opportunity to develop and grow.

After ten years with South African Breweries (now SABMiller) as human resources executive, Terry joined Barloworld Equipment, where she has been for the last fifteen years. She currently holds the position of executive director of human resources.

Terry is a warm and friendly Amiable, but her incredible strength is never far from the surface, which suggests a powerful undercurrent of Driver. She moves between the two types with ease.

As I had the pleasure of working for and being mentored by Terry early on in my career, I already knew much of her story. Shaz and I were able, once more, to focus on negotiation and the development of women.

### Why do women not get the same deal as men in business?

According to Terry, one of the key factors is that men are still the decision-makers in business. However, women do themselves no favours when they unconsciously harbour the attitudes of their mothers: 'Shouldn't I be at home with my children?'

Women do not always understand their own stereotyping and need to be more confident in making decisions that affect them personally. Terry is amazed at how women will fight tooth and nail to get a good deal for the company but, when it comes to negotiating on a personal level, they can be weak. She suspects that they don't *expect* an equal deal. This stems from the reasoning: 'How can I expect the same deal as a man when I can't stay at the office until all hours?'

Terry believes that women think that they will get ahead purely through hard work – that this alone will bring them success. But it is not always the case, and women need to define new rules for their lives. They feel guilty about working late and then shift the blame to their boss or the company. They need to set and understand their boundaries.

In Terry's experience, even women who have an equal position to men – chartered accountants, for example – still end up doing the drudge work. Men seem to appoint women when the job requires detail, probably because they are perceived to be super-efficient, as they can successfully juggle their roles as homemakers, mothers and full-time career professionals.

Like Joan Joffe, Terry feels that women need to focus more on networking. Women tend not to create the common bond that connects male colleagues. As with Joan and Kate Rau, Terry believes women should use whatever tools they have at their disposal in the business world, including persuasion and manipulation. When you get it right, she says, it is amazing how supportive men can be in helping you to rise through the ranks.

### Has there been much change in the workplace regarding gender, culture and race?

Although fundamental values and beliefs don't change much, according to Terry, people have accepted that they need to re-evaluate their attitudes and be far more flexible. As people reach new levels of maturity, positive change will happen automatically.

Terry has recently noticed that there has been a massive increase in the number of young black female applicants when she interviews for new positions in the engineering environment. Although the requirements in her last recruitment round were not colour or gender biased, many of the applicants were black females, which Terry attributes to young women being very aware of the window of opportunity now open to them. Young women today also have tremendous confidence and a desire to move up the ladder as quickly as possible. Terry finds it fascinating how these women, outside of the business environment, still have to deal with the very traditional tribal expectations their families have of them.

### Top tips to help women improve their negotiating skills

1. Know what you want. Decide how important it is to you and always maintain that level of consciousness.
2. You will have to work harder and longer than your male counterparts, but be tenacious. Although you are unlikely to get what you want through good luck, being in the right place at the right time does help.
3. Evaluate whether you are where you want to be in your life and at work. Make sure you are surrounded by people who support you.
4. You have to make conscious decisions and choices – *and* be prepared to live with the consequences.

5. Even if you don't have 'the great plan', never stop giving of your best and working hard.
6. Don't be afraid to walk away if the path doesn't suit you. It's okay to make lots of mistakes.

Without Terry's generous guidance and her faith in me in my early working career, I fear my path would have been a far more difficult one. How can a person ever repay such a debt?

## CHRISTINE WILLIAMS

Christine Williams, born in Johannesburg, is a thoroughbred Afrikaner. She takes pride in the fact that she does not possess a foreign passport. She is passionate about South Africa and being a South African.

Christine's parents assumed that she would be the next generation of medical students in her family, but, like Elizabeth Malumo, she chose not to read medicine and instead pursued studies in marketing. She graduated from the University of Cape Town (UCT) with an honours degree in business science (marketing).

While still at university Christine was recruited by Unilever, which sent her to Paris, where she spent three years in their European Innovation Office. She returned to South Africa three years later so that her husband could complete an MBA.

When Christine was young, she aspired to being the first female president of South Africa, but her subsequent experiences working with the government convinced her that most politicians are not in politics for the good of the people. So, with these thoughts in mind, Christine decided she could probably be more effective working in a big corporate, where she could concentrate on making a direct impact on the lives of others and the well-being of the organisation.

Christine is currently global director of people strategies at Standard Bank.

Although I had not met Christine before the interview, I had heard her name mentioned any number of times. She is probably a Driver with a secondary style of Expressive (same as me).

As with Shirley Zinn, Shaz and I got completely wrapped up in Christine's story.

## What burning passions have driven Christine's life and career?

Christine's father is an orthopaedic surgeon and her mother a scientist. With working parents, Christine was raised by the family's domestic helper, whom she considered a second mother. Christine spoke Sotho before she could speak English.

At a very young age, Christine questioned the different rules South Africa enforced on black and white citizens and was not able to understand why her second mother, a true matriarch, was not treated with the same respect as a white woman. Christine's strong views on this subject led her to start an underground political organisation while she was still at school.

Although a strong supporter of women's rights, Christine does sometimes feel that working women have sold themselves down the river. She is currently considering doing her PhD on the challenges working women face and how to accept that they cannot do it all.

Christine's personal values are extremely important to her, as is her very strong network of family and friends. She believes that her family and friends keep her grounded and enable her to be herself.

## Why do women earn less than men in business?

Women are not as good as men at openly discussing their expectations and often feel that hard work will get them what they want. Men are far more aggressive in pursuing what they want to earn. Christine thinks this may also be because women are driven by more than just money; for example, they want to have a positive effect on the world around them.

Gender discrimination also plays a part. Men are not always as liberal as they might seem and often don't understand the pressure on working women.

Sometimes, however, being a woman can be a great advantage. When women use the skills that are unique to them, they are more likely to achieve a deal in which both parties feel that they have got what they want.

Christine had an epiphany during a visit to China. She realised that people choose their own stress – that they have the power to make their own choices, and that they alone are responsible for achieving balance in their lives. Yet, somehow, as women, it is always the 'self' that is compromised.

## Top tips to help women improve their positions in business
1. Approach conversations from the right perspective. Don't be the victim and just say, 'I'm not happy.' Put a solution on the table when you raise a negative issue.
2. Women don't take time to reflect on their achievements. They are inclined to focus on what they have not achieved. Women spend too much time dwelling on negative factors, which means that others perceive them in a negative light too.
3. Create a 'give' versus 'get' scenario – for example, is flexibility of time more important to you than money? Decide what would be a value-for-value transaction, and then go and ask for what you want.

## DEBORAH 'DEBBIE' LEFEBVRE
I thought it would be interesting to pose the questions I had prepared to a non–South African. To this end, I coerced the delightful Debbie Lefebvre into answering them via email. Debbie is an American, and although we had never met, we struck up a wonderful cyber relationship.

In 2004, Debbie and her company, Innovative Marketing Resources, were the recipients of the Commonwealth of Massachusetts' Governor's Entrepreneurial Spirit Award. Debbie owned and operated Innovative Marketing Resources, a successful multimillion-dollar direct-marketing firm, for over a decade. A self-made and self-funded entrepreneur, Debbie took a keen interest in supporting the people in her organisation to realise their maximum potential and, rather bravely, I thought, empowered them to act as if the organisation were their own company.

After Debbie sold the company, she started a new business, DL Services Inc., which focuses on consulting to organisations across the USA on how to solve marketing and business problems. Debbie also advises on sales strategies and assists clients to reach their goals and objectives for growth, team development and overall business improvement. Debbie builds solutions using a combination of past work experiences and personal knowledge.

Debbie is currently on the board of St Leo's School and has held numerous board and volunteer positions for both civic and professional organisations.

I have now had the opportunity to meet Debbie face to face, and the passion, energy, generosity and sensitivity she communicated in her emails is exactly the diva she is in person.

Debbie is an Expressive with an Amiable leaning, i.e. a very kind, warm and communicative woman.

**Research shows that women don't get an equal deal to men in business. Is this because women are poor negotiators?**
There is still a huge inequality gap between men and women in the workplace, says Debbie, and this inequality is indeed derived from the fact that many women are poor negotiators. If women can become better dealmakers, they will be improving themselves and they will make a difference in the workplace. Women in leadership and management roles do not always know what it takes to be 'great dealmakers'.

Debbie finds it exhilarating when she sees women excelling in negotiation, especially when they are confident in what they are saying and demonstrate belief in the value of their proposals. This confidence and self-belief are not ego-driven; instead, it is a sincere self-confidence brought about by a woman's innate convictions. Debbie feels that a healthy self-esteem significantly multiplies a woman's business and personal communication abilities.

**Why are women so bad at getting what they want in a business context?**
Debbie believes that women, in general, are still subservient in the workplace and that men are the dominant players in leading roles. The sad truth is that women

seem to accept the status quo, even when they know they have the capability to perform just as well as their male peers. When women stop feeling inferior and improve their self-confidence, the workplace will become more equitable.

Debbie is convinced that it is critical for all women to invest in themselves by obtaining professional training and/or individual coaching in order to build their assurance, as well as improve their negotiating and general business skills. Women are integral in leading a company to further growth and prosperity, so why wouldn't they want to maximise their potential and performance?

### Women can be quite persuasive (or manipulative) – why does this trait not allow them to make better deals?

Women have the potential to be excellent at getting what they want, *but*, says Debbie, many seem not to know *how* to unlock the powerful skills sets that lie within them. Ironically, if they did know, they would probably feel guilty about using these abilities to their advantage! Women need to be encouraged to understand that, in harnessing these behaviours, they will serve their family, employers, customers and themselves more effectively.

### Where and how did Debbie learn her negotiating and dealmaking skills?

Debbie runs a company and doesn't have the time to think about any fear inherent in negotiating – she simply has to do it! She believes her negotiating success comes from her desire to create a positive outcome for both parties, and this applies in her personal life just as it does in business. As nurturers, women are inclined to want to please other people, and by listening to what the other person needs, women can create congruent deals.

### What was Debbie's journey? What did she do to get to the top (from a dealmaking perspective)?

Debbie says she has always focused on two things: (1) Serving others in order to create mutually beneficial deals; and (2) Using 'interpersonal intelligence' to truly understand what motivates someone else, which helps her to work cooperatively with the other party. Most women excel in these two abilities, she believes, but sometimes they lack the confidence and trust in themselves to close the deal.

## How important is 'power' in dealmaking?

When a woman is genuine, authentic and addresses the needs of the other party, she is able to increase her power. Being constructive and guiding someone else's behaviour to achieve a solution is also hugely powerful.

## Do women know what they want?
## Do they set the right goals (if any)?

Debbie feels that women should schedule more time to prepare attainable goals for accomplishing their objectives. Setting goals to alter poor behaviours and to encourage new, positive habits also helps women to perform optimally. Women are generally happy to ask lots of questions in a conversation, which encourages harmony and agreement – and they have better intuition and access to details than men!

## Top tips for women to achieve better deals

1. Connect with the person. Let him or her talk. Wait for doors to open when conversing with someone – people tend to open up when given the opportunity to do so. It's amazing what they will reveal.
2. Create a safe place – people are naturally attracted to speaking with someone who makes them feel safe.
3. Listen. Don't react.
4. Serve the other person.
5. Be genuine and authentic with yourself. Trust yourself. Take time to breathe during a conversation.
6. Prior to any important meeting or presentation, mentally visualise what you want the outcome to be. Stay positive and enthusiastic.

**Other comments on women and negotiating, selling and dealmaking**
Women are people-pleasers and are naturally excellent at serving others ... the same principles should hold true in negotiating.

It is interesting to learn that the divas across the world share the same values and attitudes when it comes to negotiation and dealmaking.

## PERSONAL GROWTH
It has been an honour for me to be in the presence of the wonderful women who were interviewed for this book. Like Shaz, I feel renewed and revitalised by the experience. I would like to thank them all, most sincerely, for their openness in sharing their stories and for their willingness to help other women to learn and grow.

I thought you might be interested to see the parallels and common threads that my team and I noticed in the interviews:
- The real-life deal divas are from a variety of backgrounds – some privileged, and some downright poor.
- Many of them have supportive husbands, but not all of them had enlightened or encouraging parents.
- They all acknowledge the negative influence that conditioning and stereotyping have had on women and their growth and development.
- Not one woman has got to where she is today through good luck. Without exception, they have all worked very hard for their success.
- They agree that women have to work harder than men to get ahead, but that hard work does not necessarily bring with it recognition. Women must tell others what they want and how they expect to be treated.
- They all concur that there is no place for high emotion in business. The best way to control emotion is to not let situations get personal.
- It is essential to be technically competent and to understand your industry and your company inside out and back to front.

- Nearly everyone recognised the power of feminine wiles and how important it is for women to use these to their advantage in business.
- None of them ever compromises their values. They always maintain their self-respect and have respect for others.
- These divine divas all want other women to succeed and are committed to helping women in every way that they can.

Take the opportunity, dear diva, to talk to the women – and men – you admire. They do not have to be more senior than you, by the way. Ask them the questions that are burning inside of you. Most people are willing to share their knowledge, and most enjoy the opportunity to show you how much they know. All you have to do is the asking. Let them guide you.

The more we can stick together and learn from one another, the closer we get to restoring women to their rightful place in the world order.

## Chapter 10

## THE END IS THE BEGINNING

> 'What we call the beginning is often the end. And to make an end is to make a beginning. The end is where we start from.'
> – T.S. Eliot
> (American-born English playwright, poet and critic; 1888–1965)

As our journey together comes to an end, and your journey as a deal diva begins, all I can do now is to encourage you to try out what you have learnt. Not everything is going to work every time, but have patience and be willing to practise, and in no time at all you will be negotiating like a pro!

If you are thinking that it would be really helpful if you could have all the lessons of the book summarised for you …

## A SUMMARY OF EVERYTHING
### Chapter 1: Are You a Diva or a Doormat?
Awareness is the first step. You need to ditch the doormat mindset and embrace the diva attitude, and you will soon be on the path to getting what you want in life.

Here are the six points you need to remember to be a divine diva:
1. You have the power to change your reality.
2. Be prepared to learn and develop yourself.

3. Take responsibility for your life.
4. Do not let discrimination and inequality get the better of you.
5. Stop saying and start doing.
6. A little self-promotion goes a long way.

## Chapter 2: Divas Get What They Deserve

Women are paid, on average, three-quarters of what their male counterparts earn. This is due, in part, to women not always being the most effective negotiators, but it is also because women calculate value differently from men.

Value for women works on three levels:

1. *How they value themselves at a very personal, individual level.*
   Women need to worry less and ask for more. When we have self-doubt, we lower our expectations of what we should earn.
2. *How women value themselves for the work that they do – what should they get paid?*
   Women do not always know their market value. This is unforgivable. Regardless of whether you are a working woman or a homemaker, you need to understand what you should be paid – in numbers.
3. *How women calculate value as part of a bigger picture.*
   When you look at the bigger picture to calculate your value, get down and dirty with the detail. You need lots of Marbles to give you the room to manoeuvre and to maintain the total value of the package you are negotiating.

## Chapter 3: From Diva to Deal Diva

We are all born with dealmaking skills, but most of us lose them by the time we are teenagers. To relearn them, we need to think like children again.

It is a good starting point to understand the differences between selling and negotiating. Selling is *persuading* the other party to accept a deal while *overcoming* objections and differences of opinion, whereas negotiating is reaching a deal through *trading* (giving to get) while *accommodating* different views and objectives.

To get what you want, you will most often persuade or trade. Persuasion doesn't always work and trading can be expensive, so consider other options before you rush in to negotiate. You can also surrender, conquer, postpone, compromise, problem-solve, resolve conflict, use arbitration or mediation, or walk away, but all of these options have costs associated with them that you can't ignore.

There are three soft areas on which you can focus to improve your confidence when you negotiate:

1. Alter your trading mindset.
2. Change your relationship with money.
3. Adjust your negotiating poise.

Avoid the four lies women tell themselves that stop them from getting what they want:

1. I am not worthy.
2. I can't sell.
3. I'm a rubbish negotiator.
4. I'm no good with conflict.

## Chapter 4: Women and the Fine Art of Communication

Communication is the imparting or exchanging of information both verbally and non-verbally. *Verbal* communication is all about written and spoken words, whereas *non-verbal* communication is predominantly body language. Verbal communication works on two levels – what we say *consciously* and what we say *unconsciously*.

The trick with *conscious* verbal communication is to choose your words very carefully, whereas what you need to watch for with *unconscious* verbal communication are the 'clues' that are inadvertently signalled. Body language is open to social and cultural interpretation, so tread carefully – but ignore feminine intuition at your peril.

The whole point of mastering communication in the context of dealmaking is so that you can make the most of your discussion time during a negotiation. Meaningless debate can lead to inconclusive or less-than-optimal deals. Constructive conversations, however, are a vital component of the dealmaking interaction.

To ensure that you maximise the time you spend 'debating' when you are doing deals, use discussion time to achieve these seven objectives:
1. Persuade and position value propositions.
2. Present (and receive) arguments to substantiate your case.
3. Test understanding and assumptions – on both sides.
4. Recap and summarise points and markers.
5. Get and give information.
6. Set expectations.
7. Test the negotiation strategy and plan.

Be sure to stay away from debate when you are in a weak position!

## Chapter 5: The Power and the Glory

There are lots of ways to create power out of nothing. Here are the six ideas we explored to increase your power base in a negotiation:
1. *Getting your negotiating gear engaged.*
   To be a powerful dealmaker, you must embrace the principle of 'give to get' as if you were a child. Power is inherent in the trading process.
2. *The power of planning – information, questions, listening.*
   **Information** – follow the four rules for using (and abusing) information:
   i. Don't invent 'facts'.
   ii. Use information to 'set expectations'.
   iii. There is an art to the disclosing or withholding of information.
   iv. Divert attention away from information that you do not want to disclose.
   **Questions** – there are three rather fun ways to extract power from questions:
   i. The quality of your questions determines the quality of the answers you receive.
   ii. Never feel uncomfortable asking for information – even sensitive information.
   iii. Interesting people are interested in others.
   **Listening** – listen, pause, think, speak. And remember the power of silence.
3. *The power of carrots.*

Carrots by any other name are really still carrots – incentives, variables, Marbles, concessions, demands, offers, hot buttons. The more carrots you have to offer the other side, the greater your power.

4. *Who really, really needs the deal?*
Power is influenced by which side needs the deal more. Obviously the party that *must* close the deal is in the weaker position.

5. *Perceptions of you – your personal authority, legitimacy, knowledge, credibility and appearance.*
Your personal authority, legitimacy, knowledge, credibility and appearance all influence your power, but the most powerful of these is … knowledge.

6. *Language and word power.*
There is only one word you need to remember – the word '*if*'. For professional dealmakers and negotiators, 'if' is the most powerful word in the dealmaking dictionary.

## Chapter 6: Being the Diva You Are Meant to Be

The answer to the question 'What role does personality play in getting the deal?' is this: Personality is not that relevant; it is *behaviour* that is important.

If you are able to determine the behavioural style of the person with whom you are dealing – *Expressive, Amiable, Driver* or *Analytical* – you will be able to tailor your persuasion and negotiation tactics to drive the expectations of the other person. Talking to someone in their own behavioural language gives you power.

Six important factors to remember in determining someone's behavioural style:

1. There are two key axes – Aggressive/Agreeable and Receptive/Sceptical.
2. Plotting these two axes to dissect one another gives you four behavioural styles – Expressive, Amiable, Driver and Analytical.
   - **Expressives:** Confident, sociable, enthusiastic, energetic, impulsive, creative, charming, persuasive, supportive, flighty, manipulative, competitive, lacking detail, undisciplined and overreactive.
   - **Amiables:** Friendly, kind, people-orientated, sympathetic, considerate,

willing, supportive, dependable, respectful, conflict-averse, unplanned, indecisive, threatened and easily intimidated.
   - **Drivers:** Direct, independent, organised, determined, focused, pragmatic, loyal, results-orientated, demanding, critical, pushy, harsh, aggressive and competitive.
   - **Analyticals:** Respectful, tactful, good listeners, obedient, persistent, industrious, logical, systematic, orderly, deliberate, organised, detailed, stubborn, cautious, tedious and somewhat anal.
3. Be aware of how your behavioural style influences the way in which you value yourself:
   - **Expressives** are great self-promoters and find it easy to establish their credibility. They must be careful not to oversell themselves relative to what they can deliver.
   - **Amiables** tend to hope that others will recognise their value and reward them appropriately. They are modest and self-effacing and, while these are admirable qualities, they need to market themselves more than they do. They need more faith in their abilities.
   - **Drivers** who use sheer force of character to demonstrate their value must realise that this is not always the best tactic. Being more gracious and less intense will help them to showcase their value to best effect.
   - **Analyticals** who are reluctant to promote themselves must realise that this does not serve them well. If they do not tell people what they are capable of, how are others supposed to know? People are not always as observant as one would hope.
4. There is no right or wrong behavioural style. Each style has its positives and negatives – or yin and yang, dark and light, good and bad – traits.
5. Adjusting your behaviour to accommodate someone else's behavioural style in order to get what you want is *not* selling out.
6. The being you are is simply and absolutely perfect.

## Chapter 7: How to Define the Deal You Want

You must go into the negotiation with a clear idea of *what* (defined deal) you want and *how* (strategy) you are going to get what you want.

*Defining* the negotiation comprises three steps:

**Step 1:** The Issues

First you need to make a list of *all* the issues that are important to the deal. Then you rank and prioritise the list, which gives you your Key Issues (big carrots) and your Secondary Issues (carrot slices, or Marbles).

**Step 2:** The Ball Park

To define the Ball Park, you need to prepare the following positions for *each* Key Issue: 'Likely', 'Bottom Line' and 'Opening'. Using the Secondary Issues, you create a list of variables with which to trade to keep the value and flexibility in the deal – Marbles you can 'get' and Marbles you can 'give'.

**Step 3:** The Players

You then decide if you are going to go into the negotiation alone or with a team. Regardless of the choice you make, there are *five tasks* that need to be performed during the meeting. The tasks are similar to those of a rugby team:

i. **Captain** – the dealmaker, leader or chief negotiator.
ii. **Vice-captain** – the translator, summariser or controller.
iii. **Coach** – the guide or observer.
iv. **Manager** – the strategist or power base.
v. **Expert Advisor** – subject-matter authority.

*Now* you are ready to negotiate!

## Chapter 8: How to Negotiate Face to Face

The top ten learning points for the face-to-face negotiating encounter are:

**1.** *There is huge power in proposals*
   You need to be able to make proposals and respond to proposals. 'If you … then I …' proposals are the most powerful of them all.

2. *Who should make the first move?*
   You! Don't get greedy and hope the other person will offer you more than you want. They are far more likely to make a proposal that suits *their* agenda. Put your Opening position on the table first if you can.
3. *Three tips for giving proposals*
   i. Present your proposals in a structured manner.
   ii. Choose your words carefully.
   iii. Be very specific when stating your conditions and offers.
4. *Three tips for getting proposals*
   i. Listen, check understanding, ask questions.
   ii. Never interrupt a proposal.
   iii. Invite them to go dancing with you.
5. *Strictly Come Dancing*
   What is the difference between a skilled dealmaker and an unskilled dealmaker? The skilled dealmaker gives the other party what they want and, in return, receives equal (or greater) value. The unskilled dealmaker, however, is the one who says 'no'. Working with an unskilled dealmaker is like a professional dancer teaching a boxer to dance – it can be done, but it ain't easy!
6. *When someone says 'no'*
   Find out why they are saying no, and ask them killer questions to test their boundaries.
7. *Should you walk away from a deal?*
   Skilled dealmakers do not generally walk away from deals. You may want to throw in the towel if:
   - Your values are being violated.
   - You are going to go below a mandated Bottom Line.
   - A long-term relationship has, or is likely to, break down.
8. *The three guidelines for engagement*
   i. **Trade** – to get you have to give.
   ii. **Trade everything** – you need lots of trading Marbles with which to trade.
   iii. **Trade everything wisely** – to get what you want, give them what they really want.

9. *When is enough enough?*
   Avoid being greedy. Recognise when you have enough and close the deal. There are *five steps* to follow to close the deal effectively:
   **Step 1** – tell them you want to close the deal.
   **Step 2** – double-check the deal.
   **Step 3** – finalise the deal.
   **Step 4** – close the deal.
   **Step 5** – sign the deal.
10. *Negotiating with loved ones?*
    Just because you are now a kick-ass negotiator, don't go beating up your friends and family. It is still okay to give them something in love!

## Chapter 9: Real-Life Deal Divas

Getting insights and advice from some of the best *real-life deal divas* is an incredible privilege. Here are the eight most important points from the interviews with these fabulous *femmes*:

1. Each woman interviewed acknowledged the negative effects that conditioning and stereotyping have had on women and their growth and development.
2. Not a single diva got to where she is today through simple good luck. Without exception, they all worked very hard for their success.
3. They all agree that women have to work harder than men to succeed, but this extra effort does not necessarily bring recognition. You must tell people what you want.
4. There is no place for emotion in business. The best way to control emotion is not to let any situation become personal.
5. It is essential to be technically competent and to understand your industry and your company inside out.
6. Nearly all the women recognised the power of feminine wiles and how important it is for women to use this trait to their advantage in business.
7. All agreed that women should never compromise their values. A woman should always maintain her self-respect and also show respect to others.

8. Every single diva interviewed wants other women to succeed and is committed to helping women make the very most of themselves.

## Chapter 10: The End Is the Beginning

If you are not sure where to start, begin with practising '*If you* do this for me, *then I* can do that for you'. You will soon discover, though, that you can't think quickly enough about what you want in return. A wonderful problem to have! This means that what you should also practise is defining your Ball Park and thinking up Marbles. Just these small steps will guarantee that you no longer get the deals of a doormat!

Here is a little confession for you: Many years ago, when the company I was working for at the time sent me to attend the Scotwork Negotiating Skills course, I was terrified. I was prepared to do anything to avoid participating in the course. My boss, Dr Karen Toombs, gave me no choice, so off I skulked. I can't say I enjoyed myself, but when it was over, I was rather pleased that I was on the path to becoming a negotiator.

Nearly twenty years on, dealmaking is finally a game. I just wish there had been a book available at the time, like the one you are holding in your hands now, which could have helped me on my way.

The next time you have to negotiate, pretend that your *Deal Diva* book is me, and take me along to do the deal with you. I have put all my positive energy and love of the subject into this book to help ensure that *you* get the best that you can out of your deals and your life.

# Pina Coladas and Cherries

'Women should be tough, tender, laugh as much as possible, and live long lives. The struggle for equality continues unabated, and the woman warrior who is armed with wit and courage will be among the first to celebrate victory.'
– Maya Angelou (American writer and poet; 1928–)

Do you realise, dearest deal diva, that this is a momentous occasion? That you are now armed with what you need to know to close the deals you want? It's time to get out the blender and all the ingredients and make the perfect pina colada. For good measure, garnish with two cherries – one for you, one for me.

And my toast to you is this: May your reign as a dealmaking diva give you everything for which you have always wished.

# References

## BOOKS

Babcock, Linda, and Sara Laschever. *Women Don't Ask: Negotiation and the Gender Divide*. Princeton: Princeton University Press, 2003.

Branson, Richard. *Screw It, Let's Do It*. London: Virgin Books, 2006.

Campbell, Don. *The Mozart Effect: Tapping the Power of Music to Heal the Body, Strengthen the Mind, and Unlock the Creative Spirit*. London: HarperCollins Publishers Ltd, 1997.

Fisher, Roger, and William Ury. *Getting to Yes: Negotiating to Agreement Without Giving In*. London: Arrow Books Limited, 1981.

Frankl, Viktor E. *Man's Search for Meaning*. New York: Pocket Books, 1985.

Jarski, Rosemarie. *A Word from the Wise*. London: Ebury Press, 2006.

Johnson, Steven. *Mind Wide Open*. London: Penguin Books, 2005.

Levitt, Steven D, and Stephen J Dubner. *Freakonomics: A Rogue Economist Explores the Hidden Side of Everything*. London: Penguin Books Ltd., 2005.

Littauer, Florence. *Personality Plus: How to Understand Others by Understanding Yourself*. Michigan: Fleming H. Revell, 1997.

Meredith, Kim. *Work Diva: How to Climb the Corporate Ladder without Selling Your Soul*. Cape Town: Oshun Books, 2009.

Orman, Suze. *The 9 Steps to Financial Freedom*. New York: Crown Publishers, 1997.

Pile, Stephen. *The Heroic Book of Failures*. Great Britain: Routledge & Kegan Paul Ltd, 1979.

Ross, George H. *Trump-Style Negotiation: Powerful Strategies and Tactics for Mastering Every Deal*. Hoboken: John Wiley & Sons, 2008.

Stimson, Tess. *Beat the Bitch: How to Stop the Other Woman Stealing Your Man*. London: Macmillan, 2009.

Wiseman, Richard. *Quirkology: The Curious Science of Everyday Lives*. London: Macmillan, 2007.

## REFERENCE BOOKS

*Collins Concise Dictionary Plus*. Glasgow: William Collins Sons & Co., 1989.

*Encarta Concise English Dictionary*. London: Bloomsbury Publishing PLC, 2001.

## MAGAZINES, NEWSPAPERS AND ARTICLES

*Business Day*, article on Jenna Clifford by Eric Webster, August 2009.

*BWA Magazine*, Summer 2008.

*Fairlady*, January 2010.

*Finweek*, 18 September 2008.

ILO, LABORSTA database, table 5B (accessed on 22 February 2005), 2005.

Mastercard Worldwide Index of Women's Advancement, July 2009.

'Rebecca West in "Mr Chesterton in Hysterics: A Study in Prejudice",' first published in *The Clarion*, 14 November 1913.

Republic of South Africa, *Employment Equity Report*, 2004.

Statistics Division of the United Nations Secretariat from International Labour Office, *Yearbook of Labour Statistics*, Geneva, 2003.

*Wits Business School Journal*, Vol. 3, 2009.

## WEBSITES

www.amazon.com

www.aquarianage.org

www.carrotmuseum.co.uk

www.en.allexperts.com

www.encyclopedia.com

# REFERENCES

www.eurofound.europa.eu
www.expressindia.com
www.goodquotes.info
www.imdb.com
www.ioljobs.co.za
www.iwf.org
www.mg.co.za
www.moneycentral.msn.com
www.nonstopenglish.com
www.noodletools.com
www.quotegarden.com
www.riotwineblog.com
www.scribd.com
www.spencerstuart.com
www.statssa.gov.za
www.thedealmaker.com
www.thefreedictionary.com
www.thesaurus.reference.com
www.unstats.un.org
www.urbandictionary.com
www.usgovinfo.about.com
www.whoswhosa.co.za
www.wikipedia.com
www.worldwidewords.org
www.yourdictionary.com